Life on the Road with the Master Wine Cellar Builder

Life on the Road with the Master Wine Cellar Builder

John Seitz

AuthorHouse™
1663 Liberty Drive
Bloomington, IN 47403
www.authorhouse.com
Phone: 1-800-839-8640

First published by AuthorHouse 08/23/2011

ISBN: 978-1-4567-9766-9 (sc)
ISBN: 978-1-4567-9765-2 (ebk)

Printed in the United States of America

This book is printed on acid-free paper.

This book is dedicated to my children, grandchildren, and my good friend John Vasel. He is the person that always told me to jot down at least a paragraph a day about my travels. Now five years later, you can read all about my journey.

About the Book

This book is about all the adventures that I have experienced in my journey to places where most people do not get to go. This is not just about all the stars and celebrities and their wine cellars but is about people, monuments, things, and places along the roads of this great country of ours.

I choose to live anywhere my motorhome will take me. I could be eating lunch in Manhattan with a friend or building a wine cellar for a star or celebrity across the country.

Sit back, relax, and enjoy your visit through the United States.

Introduction

First, I would like you to know a little bit about me. I have always been a carpenter. I started building furniture when I was about ten years old. My shop teacher told me I had a real "knack for wood." My granddaughter has a stool in her room that I built when I was around eleven years old. I would always take things apart when I was younger around twelve, thirteen years old. Most of the time I wouldn't put them back together. Anything that was composed metal and steel, even cars, I had no interest in.

One day, I guess I was about 14 years old, while in the garage I was caught by my Dad taking a lawn mower apart. I did not know that he had bought it just a few days earlier. He got so mad that I just ran out of the garage, not looking back but seeing a two-by-four board flying past me. I figured that I should stay with what I like the best—carpentry. It would probably be better for my health.

My Dad taught me a lot about carpentry when I was younger and finally took me on a jobsite where I could actually show off my carpentry skills. This didn't last too long, because as many people have learned, working for family doesn't always work out.

After serving my country in the army for three years, I traveled around the country in a semi-truck with a friend of mine delivering furniture from coast to coast. This is where the gypsy in me came out, as I look back. After traveling across the country for a year or so, I settled back to my first love: carpentry.

As the years went by I did a lot of restoring of homes in St. Louis, Missouri. I would renovate these homes back to their original condition. This was great for a while, and then that gypsy blood came back again.

Getting back to how I staterted in the wine cellar business. I built my first wine cellar for a friend who was just getting into storing wines. This was an experience that I had never known before. Not knowing anything about building wine cellars, I just went with my instincts. I did not drink wine at this time, so I built these wine cellars in the beginning for the money only. After a few years I really started to enjoy some of the wines that were given to me by my customers. They all thought that because I built wine cellars, my love of wine would be like theirs. It just goes to show that if you do something long enough you can really enjoy it.

I really enjoyed the wines we toasted the wine cellars with, some of these wines were very expensive Now this is a tradition with me. At the completion of every wine cellar that I build, the owners and I enjoy that great bottle of wine at the cellar—*their wines of course.*

Now I am consulting, designing, and building wine cellars around the St. Louis area. Something was still missing, but what could it be? I would love to travel around the country, but how is that possible?

Getting Started with The Wine Enthusiast Catalog

Maybe this was the way to do it, getting a job with a major wine cellar company in New York. I called Steve Del Duca at the Wine Enthusiast, (a catalog company in New York that sells wine cellars and wine accessories), to see if they were hiring a wine cellar installer. The immediate answer was NO. That, you would think, would be the end of it. I called again about a week later and asked the same question. Again the answer was a resounding NO. What was wrong with this guy? He didn't even know if I could do the job or not; he just simply wouldn't listen. I tried again few more times and always got the same answer: NO.

So then one day I called him up and told him that he was making a big mistake by not even listening to me. I even went as far as to tell him I was the best in the wine cellar business. That got his attention, and we had about a half an hour conversation by phone. He told me to send him some of my work and he would look at it. I knew what that meant: *no*. I didn't hear from him for quite a while, so I called him back again. Now he was not there, or so I was told. I was even more determined than ever now to get through to him. This went on for about six months before I finally got a hold of him. I asked if he had looked at the pictures of finished wine cellars I had sent him, and he said not yet. Now this guy was really bugging me. I told him to look at the pictures of the wine cellars and I would call back the next day. He said that was fine. I waited an extra day, thinking I would be cool about it. Come to find out he wasn't even there for the next few days. It took about another week or so for me to get in touch with him. By now Steve, had finally looked at my pictures of my completed wine cellars. Steve finally called me and asked me to come to New York to meet the salespeople and staff. Now I had my foot in the door and felt good about it. I put my dog, Buster, in the truck and off on a road trip to New York we went.

When I arrived at the offices of the *Wine Enthusiast Magazine*, I thought everything was just fine and figured I had a job. When could I start building wine cellars for them? I had met with the sales team and managers that morning. Steve introduced as the new wine cellar builder for the Wine Enthusiast Cataloge. We talked for about a half hour and then told me to go back home. Steve told me they would contact me if and when they had something for me to do. I didn't hear from them for a few weeks. Then the call came for me to build that first wine cellar for them.

MY FIRST WINE CELLAR FOR THE WINE ENTHUSIAST

The first wine cellar job for The *Wine Enthusiast Catalog* would be in Chicago, Illinois. By this time Steve and I had figured out that we needed a niche to stand out from everyone else. An RV would be the perfect thing. Not only would it stand out on the road, but it would especially do so when in front of someone's home where I was building a wine cellar. This would also be great advertisement for the *Wine Enthusiast,* and for me. So the first Wine Cellar RV was born.

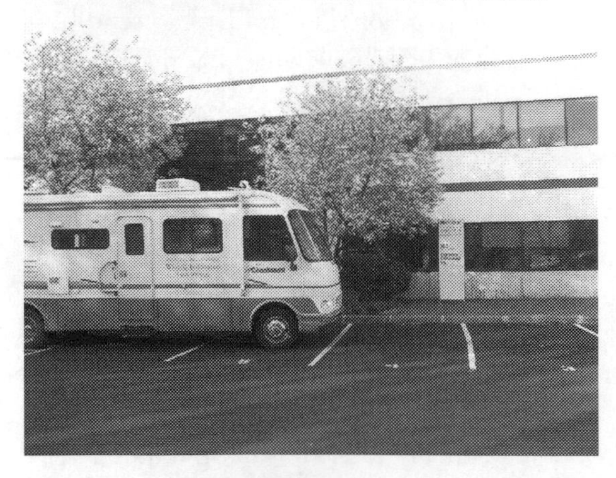

The First Wine Cellar RV

I contracted my services to the *Wine Enthusiast* catalog exclusively and soon found myself looking at the Atlantic Ocean and then the Pacific Ocean.

Traveling across this country is so intoxicating. By that I mean I also drink some of the finest wine this country has to offer. The back roads of this country are where you want to travel. There you can see the *Mayberry* towns, so small and quaint, and visit the "greasy spoon" restaurants and all the little shops down Main Street, USA. Traveling down the interstates, all you see are the billboards advertising what you could see if you were traveling the back roads.

Going back to where my first job started, my journey took me to a town outside Chicago, where I installed a wine cellar for a couple who had just begun to collect and store wine. It was in the middle of winter, and I had no idea what lay ahead for me. I left Saint Louis to go to the manufacture to pick up my racks. I had stopped off in Indianapolis for a trailer to pull behind The Wine Cellar RV. I didn't realize that pulling a trailer would be a job in itself. I drove to the manufacturing plant in Ohio to pick up the material. The sun was shining and the roads were clear. Now I am off to my jobsite. Little did I know what my future held for me and the RV.

After getting to the jobsite in Chicago, I realized that there was more to this than just putting racks together. On my previous jobs, the rooms were built by me and I knew they were square. This room was not exactly as the plans showed. The ceiling was shorter, and the width of the room was off by 1 ½ inches. Since it was my first job for a new company, I couldn't let anyone know that things may not go the way they were planned. These racks were double-deep racks, meaning that they were twenty-seven inches deep, as opposed to most racks which are thirteen and half inch. The room itself was only thirty-six inches deep.

A very small space to work in

I didn't have much room to work in. Now was a heck of a time for me to think I should have gone on a diet. I started to put these racks together, and things were going well—too well. As I looked for the connecting pieces, those famous words came to mind: Oh crap! Yes, I had put the racks together the wrong way. Not really a big deal now, as I look back on it. But at the time,this was a major disaster. You see, the customer was watching me and of course had all the confidence in the world in me. I was the wine cellar builder for The *Wine Enthusiast.* I just smiled and said as all contractors do,I blamed the factory for making a mistake. And again as all contractors do . . . I told the customer that it was not a big deal and I could take care of it. Well, those were famous last words. Nothing worked right after that. I took the racks apart and started to reassemble them.

Like I said, it wasn't pretty, in fact I broke a few pieces. I told the customer that I needed to order some more parts and would be back as soon as they came in. That was only the beginning. Halfway back to St. Louis I encountered a blizzard on the highway. I couldn't see forty feet in front of me. My only thought was to try to keep the RV in between the ditches. Finally, after what seemed like days, I made it to a truck stop. I thought the worst was now behind me. Settled in, I made some dinner and watched TV and went to sleep that night, not knowing what was ahead. I started to get a little cold but just thought that it was the wind blowing in. This was my first RV and wasn't exactly the cream of the crop. It was more like cream of the crap.

The heater on the RV went out that night. Now not only did I have to be concerned about getting heat in there to keep warm, but also now the water pipes stood a chance of freezing. Yeah, life on the road is great! The next day seemed to be a little better, though. I still had no heat from the furnace in the RV, but the sun was shining through the windows at least. The temperature outside was still below freezing. As I traveled down the highway, I was worrying about freezing pipes, and all this was on my first trip. I thought about having a little space heater going in the RV, but did I mention that the generator quit too?

I got back to St. Louis and had the heater and generator fixed, and life was supposed to be good again. This time I took my pickup truck back to the Chicago job. Things went better this time around. It was still cold, and snow was on the ground and my dog was in the back seat under some covers. While I was working on the wine cellar, I kept the motor running for heat in the truck for my dog. Finally after what seemed like the cellar was never going to be done, it was all finished. It looked good, and I was a happy camper (and wine cellar builder). The customer, his wife, and I toasted his new wine cellar, and life was good again. Now all I had to do was take that ride back to St. Louis in the middle of the night. I gave a lot of thought to what had happened and wondered if this was one of my smarter moves in life . . . hmm.

Solid redwood doors with double-deep redwood racking

My next job went a lot better. You see, the next job was in Clayton, Missouri, and was the first of many wine cellars for the Ruth's Chris Restaurant. The job had to be done at night, simply because of the union. There were two rooms to be done for a total of around 3,500 bottles.

I started the first night around 4:00 in the afternoon and quit around 2:00 the next morning. The only thing that was not as it was supposed to be was the height of the ceiling. There were some high spots, and this was an easy fix on my part. Cutting off a little bit of the racking is not a big deal, and as I found later on in my life as a wine cellar builder, salespeople, contractors, builders, or homeowners, do not always take accurate measurements. For this installation, I was in the restaurant for three nights and all went relatively well.

The last night on my way home from the jobsite, I was pulled over by a police car in the Township of Ladue. I had seen the police car on the shoulder and moved over a lane. As I passed the car and looked in the rearview mirror, the headlights and red lights came on. Not thinking too much about it, I just kept going. Then the realization came that the car was after me. The officer asked me for my license and insurance card and asked me if I had been drinking. The officer said I had swerved back there on the highway. I told her I just moved over when I saw the police car on the side. After about a half an hour of conversation, she let me go and told me to drive carefully. I just think she was bored on that stretch of highway and wanted something to do. Be careful if you drive Interstate 64 at two or three o'clock in the morning. Check out the Ruth's Chris Steakhouse when you are in the Clayton area in St. Louis. This was another job under my belt for the *Wine Enthusiast*, and now it seemed like it was a good idea to run around the country in The Wine Cellar RV building wine cellars.

Ruth's Chris Steakhouse, Clayton, Missouri

My next out of town job

One job in Florida proved to be somewhat of a challenge. The entrance to the street was very small. Being new to RVing, I wasn't quite sure if I could make it in there. Once inside the gates, the trees and a narrow street proved to be more of a challenge. The Wine Cellar RV was getting scratches on both sides from the trees.

The wine cellar was to be constructed in a small room off an office. On this job I had to tear out the existing drywall, reframe a partial wall, drywall with new green board, and mud, tape, and paint the walls. Since I was by myself, this may have been too much for me to handle. I went to the local manpower company to try to get some help lined up. This is something that I would never want to again do. The people whom they sent to my jobsite were not prepared to work at this job; they had not had a bath in a while either. I sent them back right away. I then found some local carpenters to help me with the job, and all seemed to go well.

The second day on the job, the sun was shining and it was getting a little warm in The Wine Cellar RV. My dog, Buster, was in there and needed to be comfortable, so I fired up the generator, turned on the house air conditioner, and went back to work. About an hour later I came back outside and did not hear the generator running. I went into the RV, started up the generator, and as I looked out the window, I saw oil all over the driveway. When I had checked the oil the night before, I had not put the dipstick in the engine very tightly. You learn so much out here, and sometimes not in a very good way. After about an hour, I got everything cleaned up and went back to work. Now the customer must have been thinking that he might even have to put down some wood shavings on the oil to soak it up a little. After about four days of working, his wine cellar would be complete. When I had finished installing the door on the wine cellar, the customer wanted me to install his door handle also. This is something your local locksmith would normally do. With all that went wrong, I thought I would be nice and do this for him. The customer had the wrong locks for the door. It would almost seem this was my fault too. It is a job for a locksmith, not a wine cellar builder.

Custom wine cellar in Florida

I went on to my next job, which was at Kiawah Island, South Carolina. I figured that since the RV had just come out of the shop, everything would surely go smoothly now. Everything was running fine till one morning when I woke up and reached down to pet my dog lying next to the bed. He was wet, and I thought that he had an accident in the middle of the night and now I had a mess to clean up. I felt sorrier for my dog than I did for me cleaning up the mess. Well, when I came through the winter storm, I had a water line break. Funny how I was just finding out about it a month later. I found a Home Depot to get some plastic lines and went to work. The water lines used in RVs are not standard lines. I had to replace about forty feet of water line to get it to stop leaking. As I traced the leak through a wall, I found out I had picked up a hitchhiker somewhere along the line. A mouse had come in and made himself at home. He had built a home out of toilet paper, had morsels of dog food next to his bed, and of course had left mouse poop all over the place. This life on the road in an RV can be horrible. I never pictured all this up and down in just a couple of months of being on the road. Finally, after a couple of days of working on the water lines and getting the mouse poop out, I was ready to roll again.

When arriving at my job in Kiawah Island, I found that it was a huge place. I asked the builder why when someone builds a huge home like this you would let someone else build a two-story home so close to the house. His reply was, "That is the guest house!" Open mouth, insert foot. The job was a small one right off the kitchen, housing about three hundred bottles. The racking was dark stained with a tabletop and a place to hang wine glasses. It took me a couple of days to complete this wine cellar. Everyone thought it went pretty fast.

Off the kitchen in Kiawah Island, South Carolina

I built a wine cellar in Virginia where the owner had an indoor tennis court, swimming pool, and a bowling alley (not just one, but two alleys). When I asked him why two alleys, his response was "I would not want my guests to wait." Life is tough! Talking with some of the other contractors on the job, I found out that the owner had spent about one million dollars on a security system so far.

The wine cellar was right off the main hallway on the lower level. There were iron doors to get into the wine cellar. The walls and ceiling were covered with brick coming to points. One side of the wine cellar consisted of racks just for cases. This wine cellar took me about four days to put together. A lot of my wine cellars that are built involve more than just putting racking together. There has to be knowledge of what goes together and why, as well as the weight of bottles, size of bottles.

After I left the jobsite, The Wine Cellar RV again screwed up. I was in a parking lot, watching TV, when everything in the RV just quit working. I had just gotten it out of the shop. When I called them to see what I could do to get things going again, they replied, "What did you do to it this time?" I know they said that as a joke, but I was not laughing. This was certainly not the response I was looking for. Anyway, it turned out to be a gigantic fuse hidden away under the fender—like people really know there is a fuse there. Some very nice people at a Ford dealer found the problem and now everything was working again. I decided that I'd better leave well enough alone and get rid of this. That's just exactly what I did. There is a lot more to these motor homes than you would think. I was finding out that this was a house going down the road bouncing around, and things just break.

When I got back to St. Louis Missouri, I went to Apache Village RV Center and traded the old one in for a newer one. Of course I learned my lesson from the first one. That's why I bought the second one from a different dealer than the first. This one was really nice and had two slide-outs and a lot of room. This was also the one that was published in the *Wine Enthusiast* magazine. From then on this RV would be known as The Wine Cellar RV. This RV was a very recognizable vehicle when traveling down the road. There were pictures of wine cellars on the side and back. Now people were waving and saying hello to me all over the country. I felt like a celebrity.

The first time I drove the second Wine Cellar RV with all the logos upon it to the *Wine Enthusiast* offices in New York, everyone who looked at the new vehicle was amazed at the difference between the two.

The second Wine Cellar RV

A wine cellar job in Kansas City, Kansas, was another memorable one for me. It was a small job in a very unique place. The front of the wine cellar was glass from top to bottom, and it had a full light in the door for the entrance. This was right off the living room, which made it different. I did not get a chance to finish the whole cellar, because I was missing some parts. This time it was not my fault!! I ordered the parts I needed from the factory and told them I would be back there in a couple of weeks. I drove back to St. Louis Missouri for a while, but soon I was ready to leave. This was a time when you didn't worry about your fuel bills. I drove back to Kansas City to finish the job. This took me a couple of days and I was off again to another adventure.

I left Kansas City and thought, *Where do I want to go?* Like I said earlier, fuel was not that much of an expense at this time. I started to travel south, since this was wintertime. I ventured out along I-35 in Kansas and down into Oklahoma. Outside of Oklahoma City, I looked at something along the roadside. As I got closer, it appeared to be someone lying on top of a bike. I slowed down a little because I didn't want to startle the guy. He didn't move. I went to the next exit and turned around and came back. I still didn't see any movement. As I got closer, I pulled over on the shoulder. I got out of the RV and yelled at the guy, "Are you okay?" Well, he really wasn't—the man was dead. I called the local police department. They came out and got him. It amazes me that no one had stopped to see if this man was okay. The police officer said he had been dead for quite a while.

As I went on with my journey I wondered how long it would be before someone discovered me if I died out here on the road. Would they drink the wine? Eat the food on board? Hopefully they would read my book while sipping on fine wine.

As my journey took me out across Oklahoma, I was going to spend the night at the local Flying J truck stop. Still being fairly new to this RV lifestyle, I found out that some of the truck stops don't accommodate RVs. This truck stop was noisy and the weather in the area wasn't looking so hot, so I decided to go just a little further. There was an RV park that I knew of down the road about seventy-five miles, where there would be some shelter from the bad weather coming in.

The place I stopped at was the Best Western RV Park and Motel in El Reno, Oklahoma. When I pulled in there, they were glad to see me again. They looked at the RV and saw that it was a different one from before. After I checked in they told me that there was a tornado alert for the area. They put me in a place that would be out of the biggest part of the wind. That night a tornado hit all around the area, but the next morning the sun was out and it was a beautiful day to travel. Now I am glad I did not stop at the truck stop. The motel next to the RV Park served a great breakfast that morning, and then I was off to California.

On my way out there was another landmark that I wanted to stop at: the Texas Steakhouse. Here they serve up a seventy-two ounce steak, and if you can eat it all in an hour, you don't have to pay for it. Well, you do pay for it, just at a later time, along with stomach cramps and everything that comes along with it. Needless to say I wound up paying for my meal, because there was no way in the world that I could eat that much food in an hour. Now that I was stuffed I went to the Amarillo Ranch RV Park in Amarillo, Texas, and just relaxed for a while. The next day also turned out to be great. The sun was shining and all was back to being a day that would be memorable.

Steakhouse in Amarillo, Texas

As I traveled across the state of New Mexico, a lot of good things happened along with some not-so-good things. As I was getting fuel, some people came up to me and asked me if I was John Seitz. I answered, "Yes I am." They said that they were always looking for The Wine Cellar RV but never thought they would see it. One man handed me a catalog for me to sign. I gave them a couple of CDs, and everyone enjoyed some of the stories I told them. Before I got a chance to leave the fuel stop, one of them came back with a bottle of wine from a local winery for me. People can be really nice sometimes. This was written into the Wine Enthuiast by Randy

> **Randy said:**
> **August_4th,_2009_at_2:57:48_PM**
> Ran into John off of I-40 in Tucumcari NM. He was on his way to cali. NICE ride . . . The CD really shows some cool projects before and after . . .

Later on that week my slide-out wasn't really working as well as it should have. I was stopped one night and put out the slide-out as usual, not thinking anything of it. The next morning when I tried to bring it back in it wouldn't come in. I went outside to see if I could see anything there, and the man next to me asked if he could help. (People in RV parks are always there to lend a helping hand.) It took a little bit, but between the two of us we finally got it back in.

My next place to visit was the RV shop, again. The guy said he could get me in right away. I went into the waiting room with some other customers. There was a magazine that one of the customers was reading, and it just happened to have me in it. They looked at me for a little bit and asked if it was me. I told them what I do and showed them a few pictures of some wine cellars I had built. They were very impressive, they said. Not as impressive as the bill I would get later.

I was there for about eight hours and was bored out of my mind. The RV was just about done. The service manager came out to tell me he was ready for me now. They ran a new wire about ten feet, and I was charged almost $1,000. This RVing is expensive. Going from shock to reality, I paid the bill. Now I wanted to find someplace to spend the night. The RV park put me in a space that really wasn't big enough for me, but it was a quiet place to spend the night. The next morning was sunshine and blue skies. A perfect day for driving.

When driving through Arizona I stop of at my of my favorite RV Parks, Zuni Village RV Park. This is what they had to say about me.

> **Verna McCumber said:**
> **June_22nd,_2008_at_7:17:12_PM**
> Your man John stopped by to stay over with us here in Kingman,AZ. at Zuni Villiage RV Park on his way to S.F.,CA. and again on his return trip back home. It was a pleasure meeting Mr.Seitz and I look forward to seeing him if he's ever this way again.
> ~~~~Mr.John Seitz I want to thank you again for the autoghraphed magazine and wine you gave me and hope you have a safe trip back home.~~~~Verna McCumber

I arrived in California, the first time I had been there in a long time. I had an onsite to do outside of Los Angeles and went to the house to see how large a wine cellar we could build. They were going to turn their son's room into a wine cellar. Great, but what if the son wanted to come back home? I took some measurements and gave them some ideas and went on my way.

Just wait till his son comes home to find a wine cellar

After leaving California, I decided to just follow the coast south. I drove all along California's Route 1 and into Arizona. I then went across New Mexico and down into Texas. The views from some of the hills were spectacular. I saw a couple of signs stating that there had been UFO activity in the area. Now I had spaceships on my mind, and this played a big part on the trip through southwestern Texas. I drove along the Rio Grande River and was amazed at the scenery. In the distance I saw what looked like a UFO to me. Like I said, I had spaceships on the brain. I kept looking at this thing in the air and a few times almost ran off the road. Good thing there was no one around me for miles. I just kept staring at this object in the sky. I didn't want to call the police and look like a fool. But what was this thing? I got closer and closer and still couldn't figure it out. You have to understand that the area I was in had UFO sightings a lot. Could I actually be seeing a UFO? I broke down and called the police and told them I was seeing something in the sky and it was not moving. The response I got was not exactly a favorable one. They said they would check it out. Yeah right! I was in the middle of nowhere and they would check it out. Finally I was close enough to get a picture of this thing. Was I now staring at a real UFO? My heart was pounding harder and harder. Would I be abducted by this thing? There was no sound. It was motionless, and I needed to get closer to take a picture. I got my camera out, stood behind the door of the RV, and zoomed in on it. *Not a UFO!* It was a weather balloon. The shape of it was like a child's toy. Now I felt very foolish and wanted to get out of there before the police came out to investigate.

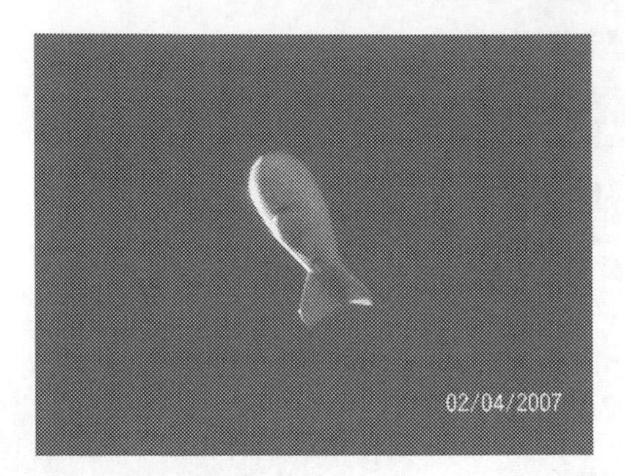

Doesn't this look like a UFO?

I had the pleasure of meeting Robert Redford at a gas station in Nevada. I was filling up The Wine Cellar RV with fuel. This was of those days when I did not want to talk to anyone, much less meet a movie star. A voice came from behind me and said, "You're The Master Wine Cellar Builder, aren't you?" I was going to be a smart ass, with a remark like "That's what it says on the RV." Then the guy lifted his sunglasses, and when I looked at him I knew it was Robert Redford. I said, "You're Robert . . . ahh," and he interrupted and said Redford. My reply was "No, that's not it." (I was just messing with him.) The look on his face was not good, and he almost seemed to be insulted by my comment. After a couple of minutes, I finally said I knew who you were all along. He just smiled, and we talked for a while. Now Robert Redford has my business card with him. It was a treat for me to be recognized by a big movie star.

I remember one time when I was building a wine cellar in Illinois. Not thinking too much about whom it belonged to, I just went on about my business. After getting set up, I took all the measurements of the room, checked out my drawing of the racking, and started to build the wine cellar. Walking in and out of the room I looked at some of the items on the bar and shelves. I saw a lot of McDonald's Hamburger items there. Then later on in the day a man came down to say hello. I figured it was the homeowner, and we started talking about his new wine cellar and wine. I asked him, since I saw all this McDonald's stuff, whether he owned one of the franchises. His response was that he was the CEO. Oh, like a manager of a franchise,I said? He looked at me again and spelled it out: C-E-O. I felt a little dumb at that point. I told him that it was kind of ironic that after all these years of spending money at McDonald's for my kids and grandkids I was now getting some of it back building a wine cellar for him. He just smiled and laughed a little bit. The wine cellar was off the main part of the lower level. You could see the bottles in there through the window and the glass in the door.

I met John Schneider (from *The Dukes of Hazzard*) at the KOA campground in Anderson, South Carolina. I was on my way out of the campground but was stopped by an RV with a trailer blocking the road. I was walking toward the door of the RV when the door opened and John Schneider appeared from behind it. I was a little startled when I said, "You're John Schneider," and his reply was, "You're John Seitz." I found out later that he had looked up the website printed on The Wine Cellar RV. He said they got in late last night and was sorry for blocking the exit. He was on tour promoting his latest movie. We were talking a little bit, and he asked to see the inside of The Wine Cellar RV. He was touring the country in an Alfa See Ya motor home. We were discussing wines and wine cellars when he asked me to recommend a fine wine for him. I did better than that—I went to my personal wine collection and handed him a 1998 Cabernet. Then I asked him if I could take his picture at the back of The Wine Cellar RV.

John Schneider

I thought it was pretty nice of him to do this, since he hadn't shaved yet and was just in a T-shirt. I guess he felt comfortable going back to his *Dukes of Hazzard* days.

I went to Las Vegas to do an onsite wine cellar consultation on one of my trips. This was no ordinary onsite, I found out. The owner had brought in people from all over the world to build his condo overlooking Las Vegas Nevada. The view was great from the condo, which occupied two floors. One of the floors housed a hot tub that looked like a giant wheel on a roulette table. The wine cellar itself would house only about six or seven hundred wine bottles. This was one of those homes that would be a for a weekend getaway only. My weekend getaways consisted of being invited to stay in a guest room when I visited someone around the country.

View from the condo in Las Vegas

While I was in Las Vegas I thought I would do a little sightseeing. I was only one mile from the RV park and had an accident right there while waiting at a red light. I was struck from behind by a pickup truck and then pushed into the car in front of me. Good thing I was in a rental car and not The Wine Cellar RV. The man who struck me said that he just did not see me. The car rental people didn't say anything when I got back with the crunched-up car. They gave me another one and I was on my way. A few weeks later I had some paperwork delivered to me and they wanted me to pay $12,000 to repair the car. I called them and reminded them that the police report stated that I was not at fault. I was hit from the rear. Sometimes people just don't read the whole story and try to just take the easy way out.

When I was traveling along a secluded highway in Oregon, I saw a huge bird flying around me when I was doing about sixty-five miles an hour. The bird came directly at me, and next I heard a crash. The bird hit my satellite dish. As I looked out the window, I saw the dish hit the side of the road, smashing into pieces, and then I saw the bird that had been circling me fall to the side of the road. Judging by the sound the crash made, I knew there was not I thing I could do for the bird or my dish. Good thing I didn't subscribe to the Dish Network. Sometimes you are just at the wrong place at the wrong time.

From the middle of nowhere a bird appears

Driving along the Snake River is a beautiful view. The river running alongside of the highway where you see a lot of Jet Skis. When watching these people going back and forth across the river, you almost forget that you need to watch the road yourself. That happens quite a bit when traveling.

I finally made it to Portland, Oregon, to do my next wine cellar. Just like I have seen so many times since then, the room was not ready for me to start the job. I would have to wait a few days before the room would be done and I could install my racking. This was not to be the first time that I had to wait, and certainly not the last. I checked into the Portland RV park right outside of Portland. My view from the park was that of Mt. Rainier. Of course I could only see it when it quit raining. The days I spent there were mostly inside the RV, only going out when my dog needed to.

Then I received the call that the room was finally ready, I spent three days on the construction of the wine cellar. There were still things that needed to be done by the carpenters while I was in the wine cellar.

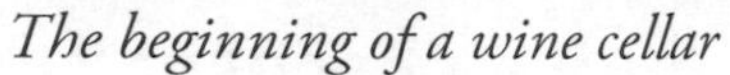

The beginning of a wine cellar

UPS delivering my product

Upon completion on my part, it was time to toast the wine cellar with the owner and his wife, which we did with some of Oregon's finest wine.

Leaving the jobsite, again not knowing where I wanted to go, I decided to drive down the coast of Oregon, a beautiful hiway, and I had a chance to drink some more of Oregon's wine. I stopped overnight at the Chinook Winds Casino and had a great breakfast buffet the next morning.

Whenever traveling, I always try to take the side roads. There is so much more to see when you are off the main highways. Getting into California, I saw where Bigfoot was supposed to be and lots of "real Bigfoot stuff." It's amazing all the things that this mythical creature has brought onto the market. From there I had a chance to see the tall redwoods in northern California. There are trees tall enough and split in the middle such that you can drive a car through. Traveling down the road the cell phone connection was difficult at times. Neither my cell phone nor the Internet connection worked until I arrived in Santa Rosa, California.

Whenever I travel in California, I like to take Highway 101. The road is a great road to do some sightseeing from. Sometimes the clouds coming over the mountains are breathtaking. You don't just see that anywhere. It is amazing that just a few hours apart you can have the ocean or the mountains.

Since I like to travel Highway 101 in California, I have met some interesting people. I was at a rest area on Highway 101 when Jay Leno came up to The Wine Cellar RV and was just looking. Jay Leno is interested in anything on wheels. I saw him and went outside to talk. We talked for about fifteen minutes. He seemed to be very interested in what I did. When I told him I build wine cellars for a lot of stars and celebrities, he said he had never heard of anyone doing that before, especially driving around the country in a motor home. He told me that I was very interesting and that when I knew that I was going to be in the Los Angeles area, I should stop in and he would put me on the show. That was very exciting. I was thinking about that for the next few days.

When I drove back to Santa Rosa California to do my next job, I parked The Wine Cellar RV at the Wal-Mart parking lot, a lady came up to me and asked for my autograph as she flipped to the picture of me in a *Wine Enthusiast* catalog she had received. This was one of many times when I would be asked. It felt really special.

The wine cellar job in Santa Rosa I learned that I couldn't bring The Wine Cellar RV all the way to the house. The roadway seemed almost too small for a good-sized pickup truck. So I got as close as I could and the customer took my tools and me the rest of the way in his car. Again these are the things that you never think about but will encounter again and again. I built this wine cellar in a round room that brought more challenges that I had ever known before. I am now finding out that the wine cellars I had built before were very simple compared to this one.

My next job would have me traveling across the south to New Orleans was certainly an experience in its own. This was after Hurricane Katrina, and people were still trying to get their lives back together again. Some of the main streets were intact. Going down Bourbon Street was an eye-opener. I don't think I had ever been down this street before in my life. The Holiday Inn Hotel had a giant clarinet on the side of it. That was an interesting thing to see.

Check out the clarinet on the side *Bourbon Street*

My onsite in New Orleans was for a man who wanted to have a wine cellar in an old slave house. The walls were concrete and brick, not insulated, and also had too many windows or doors. The guy wanted to keep this place as close to the original as possible. I told him to just stick a wine cooler in there and forget about making it into a wine cellar.

Where should the wine cellar be? After the consultation, the customer agreed that the best solution would be just a chiller. This way the integrity of the room would still be intact.

Before leaving the area I drove around a bit more just to do some sightseeing. Why waste a day and the cost of a rental car? The trolley train looked like it was on the wrong side of the street, but it came down the middle of the street. The River Walk was another interesting place to walk around. The shops and restaurants were amazing.

Trolley Train *River Walk*

When building wine cellars in and around our nation's capital, Washington, DC, I could not take The Wine Cellar RV into the small townships. I stayed at Cherry Hills RV Park in Cherry Hills, Virginia. Renting a car and going back and forth proved to be a job in itself. The roadways around Washington, DC, seemed to always be crowded. Taking the beltway in the morning did not bother my dog Buster at all.

Buster being chauffeured to the jobsite

This job took about three days to do, and every day Buster would just sit in the backseat looking out the window.

My next job would take me out to California again. I had a wine cellar to build in San Jose. My daughter Colleen, who was 24 years old, went with me on this trip, which had an interesting start. Everything was packed the night before so we could take off early and just have a relaxing trip. I was looking forward to spending some time with my daughter. As we approached the highway my engine temperature was on the rise. I pulled over in a parking lot to find out what this was. There was a split in the heater. I replaced the hose and was going to head back home and start out again in the morning, but when I started the engine, there was still a leak from somewhere. Well, the hose that I replaced had been split, but there was another one next to it also split. After getting all fixed, I decided to head back home and get cleaned up before we ventured out again.

Now it was early afternoon and we were on the road. Colleen was sitting back in The Wine Cella RV, watching the ball game and enjoying her beer while going down the road. The first night we stopped north of Kansas City, Kansas. We made dinner and watched a little television, and I relaxed after a long day. Going across the country, my daughter slept during the day, (early morning) and enjoyed the scenery after she woke up. She was amazed at all the people who were honking at us and waving. (Remember that it said "Master Wine Cellar Builder" on the side of The Wine Cellar RV.)

We were going to stop at one RV park but then decided to go on a little farther down the road, after looking up at the sky.

The weather was clouding up, and we found out later that a tornado was headed our way. We ducked in a place that would be safe for the night. After a night of high winds and lots of rain, the next day would prove to be beautiful again.

Colleen and I stopped off at a few wineries along the way. She was surprised at how many people knew me. We tasted wines from the barrels and had wines not available to the public yet. As I normally do, we traveled the back roads, and Colleen was amazed at all the vineyards along the road. We went to Windsor California, to do a quick job for a builder. This was the first time I was ever asked to just put the racking together and not install it. It took me only a few hours and we were on our way again.

Trying to let Colleen see as much of the coast as I could, we took California Highway 12 to Highway 1. This is not a road that you want to take an RV on. Of course, I didn't find this out until it was too late. The road was lined with trees leaning across the roadway. But we did find little shops and eateries in these small towns along the way. After leaving the towns, the fun part came in, as the roads seemed to have gotten smaller and narrower. On the one side, the mountains seemed to never stop as you looked up. On the other side was the ocean, with a cliff almost straight down.

Almost straight down

After I unclenched my hands from the steering wheel, we were almost down the side of the mountain and ready for a break. The road would wind back and forth. Sometimes it seemed too small for the RV and a car to be on the road at the same time. I think some of the people in the car would look up at me and pray that I would not run them off the road. I have not been back on that road since, especially now that I have a bigger RV. We stopped off at the beach and walked around for a while. It was a little chilly, so it wasn't good for swimming. There was a sign on the beach about sharks, that I had never seen before.

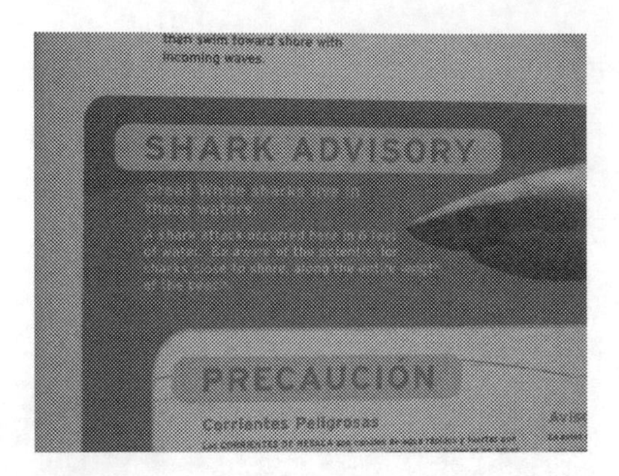

Do you think they have Spanish-reading sharks also?

After leaving the beach, we both decided that we needed a cold beer and a hot steak. We found a restaurant outside San Francisco along the coast with great steaks and plenty of cold beer.

The next day when we arrived at the jobsite in San Jose, I began to do what I do best. Let's see, where do I begin? It would always take me a little bit to get everything together. I had a cooling unit to install in this wine cellar. I had to cut out a hole in the wall and not get too much drywall dust around. Since I had my daughter with me on this job, she could help me with the cleanup. Colleen was out in the RV still sleeping—I guess some things never change. After getting up she came in to help me with the wine cellar; I enjoyed having my daughter with me.

We stayed at a new Coyote Valley RV park about an hour south of the jobsite. Traffic going through San Jose was very slow. The RV park had a swimming pool and grocery store and very nice people who ran the place. Colleen and I would barbecue, drink wine, and just relax. After about three days, we were done with the cellar and Colleen was about ready to go home. I guess two and half weeks on the road was enough for her. This is one of the benefits of having a job like mine. I can have my family with me to enjoy some of this country's finer things. I took Colleen to the airport and went off on my next adventure. As she flew back to St. Louis, I would venture down the interstate.

As you probably figured out by now, I never have any particular route to go. I decided to travel on Interstate 80, across the country, and then take a detour to Utah and across Interstate 70. I saw something on this trip I had never seen before, the Arches National Park in Utah. The arches are so spectacular, the size of the rock formation. When you stand at the bottom and look up, they are so huge that they never seem to stop as they go on into the sky. The people standing at the bottom of the arches seem to be very tiny. Can you imagine years ago when dinosaurs roamed in this area? They probably didn't think the arches were that big, just a place to get out of the sun.

The Arches in Utah

The day that I had to put Buster down was one of the worst days of my life. I had now lost my best friend. The night before, Buster had been out playing and running around. We were on the way to the next jobsite when Buster let out a yelp like I have never heard before. He never complained about anything, so I knew something was wrong. I pulled over to the side of the road, and he was just listless. This was not the energetic dog I knew. We went to the nearest vet, and they took x-rays and his blood count, neither of which was very good. I called his vet back home and told him what was wrong. He told me it was time. My heart just sank thinking that I would not have Buster with me anymore. I never thought that was our last day together would have been yesterday. After six months of cancer treatments, there was no more hope. We had spent twelve and a half years together. I remember my daughter picking him out from a litter. He weighed about three pounds and looked like a tiny bear cub. Now I wouldn't have him with me anymore. The first night without him was so lonely; all I could do was think about him the night before. My youngest daughter, Mary Lauren, flew out to be with me. One is always glad to have family at a time like this.

In memory of Buster, 1995-2007

Scenes from around the country

Traveling around the country as I do, a person gets to see more than the vast majority of Americans ever get to see. From the Golden Gate Bridge in San Francisco to Times Square in New York, the following pages are just a few more of the sights around this great nation of ours.

Times Square, New York

Cadillac's buried in the ground outside Amarillo, Texas

Hoover Damn outside Las Vegas

Johnny Depp giving an interview in Las Vegas

The Las Vegas Strip

World's largest thermometer

Spaceship house in Arizona

Traveling in a tunnel under the Gulf Coast in Alabama

Truck carrying bombs in San Antonio Texas (not live bombs)

Propeller for wind turbine

Louisiana swamp along Interstate 10

Shuttle launch from Cape Kennedy

Border patrol in Arizona

Beautiful view along Highway 1 in California

The Golden Gate Bridge in the fog

Space Needle in Seattle, Washington

Looks like a real whale; entrance to casino

Balloon taking off in Aspen, Colorado

Articles and tips on Wine Cellars

Here are some of the articles written by me for Celebrity Wine Review TV.

All about Wine Cellars, Part One

So you are thinking about a wine cellar.

A lot of questions come to mind, and you're not sure of which way to go.

- Where do I even start?
- How big of a wine cellar do I want?
- Do I want an active wine cellar?
- Do I just want a wine room?
- Do I just want a wine chiller?
- Where do I go to get some answers to these questions?

Let's start off with another question . . .

Are you a wine drinker who likes to drink the wine that you buy right away, or do you plan on buying wine for consuming now and then saving some for later?

Are you the wine drinker who will buy wine for an investment?

Do you buy wines by the case or individual bottles?

What size bottle do you buy your wine in?

- Splits 375 ml
- Bottle 750 ml
- Magnum 1.5 liter
- Jeroboam 3.0 liter
- Imperial 6.0 liter

Now some of you may be thinking, *Why not just store wine in my closet?* My answer to that is that anytime you store bottles of wine at improper cellar temperatures, your wine will always be inferior to a bottle stored to peak at the correct temperature 55-57 degrees, 70% humidity, period. So why would you want to spend all that money just to open that bottle of wine for a special occasion and wind up with vinegar?

There are a few other questions to ask yourself before you even talk to your wine cellar builder. One of those questions is "Where in the heck do I build my new wine cellar?" The most logical place you would think is in the lower level of your home. Not bad, so let's start there. Do you have a corner that can be used for your new wine cellar? This would actually be the best. You could build your wine cellar in any room of your home as long as you go through the proper building procedure. Wine does not like a lot of light, noise (which causes vibration), or anything that would irritate the wine (various odors, paint, etc.).

With all these questions in your mind, you need to ask the experts. In the next few articles we will cover the answers to these and more of your questions.

John Seitz
Master Wine Cellar Builder
Any questions please e-mail john@celebritywinereview.tv

This article is about the importance of venting your wine cellar's cooling system. Let's discuss the effects it could have on your wines, wine cellar, and of course the cooling equipment itself. Whether you are using a forced air system through the wall starter unit or a more sophisticated split or air handler, they all need to be vented properly and need to follow the same guidelines.

There are a lot of misconceptions about how to vent a cooling system. I am going to touch on the proper conditions needed. I will also discuss issues that will fall into those areas of concern that should be red-flagged, meaning that there needs to be further discussion before using them. These red-flagged areas meet much of the definition of a proper area for venting but also contain elements unique to their own conditions that could potentially cause problems, so they need to be looked at thoroughly before being considered.

First let's discuss how important venting correctly really is. I want you to take a moment and imagine running up a flight of stairs in your home as fast as you can and then at the very top of the stairs stepping inside the coat closet full of coats and other items and trying to catch your breath. Sounds impossible, right? More than likely you won't be able to and you would have to come out of the closet to where there is a greater abundance of fresh cool air for you to regain your breath. It is the same for a cooling unit venting into a similar area or one that is just too small.

Venting directly to the outdoors using a cooling unit intended for indoor venting is asking for disaster. Outdoor conditions are too extreme for the cooling unit to perform properly, again inviting disaster. Outdoor venting should be left to those cooling systems with outdoor condensers. This time I want you to imagine what it is like to jog on a hot summer day or in the frigid winter. How will you perform at your best? Your performance would be impeded either way. These analogies are the same for a cooling unit, and they experience similar results. In addition, cooling units rated for indoor venting are not rated to operate under rainy conditions and could potentially short out the unit, causing greater problems than just the unit failing.

Now let's get to the nitty gritty of how important proper venting of the cooling unit is. Venting is the most overlooked and underestimated design element of building a wine cellar but actually is one of the most important, if not the most important, next to the wine cellar buildout. Without it, everything has been done in vain.

If you have ever shopped for a forced air/through-the-wall cooling unit, you more than likely have been told that the cooling unit needs to vent through the wall into the adjacent interior air space, which needs to be twice the size of the wine cellar, and the temperature should not exceed 75°F. Seems simple and easy enough that anyone can do it. This is a very broad statement and can lead you down the path of disaster.

So what would happen if the space was not large enough to dissipate the hot air exhaust? Keep in mind that these cooling units could be discharging temperatures of 95°F into the venting area and the heat would continue to increase using its own exhaust to try to cool down the hot condenser with air 95°F or higher. Remember running outside in the heat? How does that affect your performance? Same with the cooling unit. First, it will not be able to hold temperature since these cooling units are generally built to work off a twenty—to thirty-degree temperature differential, meaning that if the temperature inside the cellar is 55°F, the maximum temperature outside should not exceed 85°F. As the temperature rises outside the cellar, it will exponentially increase inside the cellar, which is not good for your wines. All the while it will be working harder, thus prematurely shortening the life of the condenser. I have seen this many times, and it is a very common occurrence that can be corrected. If not, you will be replacing cooling unit after cooling unit and always at the most inconvenient times, like during the heat of the summer months.

Earlier on I mentioned that there are interior spaces that meet most of the definitions of a space to vent to but are red flags and need to be discussed further to determine if they are appropriate for this use. In review, what we are looking for is an interior space equal to or greater than the maximum cooling capacity of the cooling unit, and the temperature shouldn't exceed 75°F.

The following are some places that may not be the best for venting you cooling unit into:

1. **Closets and pantries:**

These need to be free of any clothing or storage to keep the exhaust from the cooling unit building up inside. The cooling unit will draw in own exhaust.

2. **Crawl spaces:**

Crawl spaces are generally dirty and difficult to get in to clean and maintain the cooling unit properly. They tend to be very stagnant and not allow the exhaust to dissipate but to linger around the cooling unit, allowing the cooling unit to draw back in its own exhaust to cool itself down. In most new construction, the crawl spaces are hermetically sealed and made air tight to keep out unwanted rodents, and this makes it worse for venting into.

3. **Mechanical and boiler rooms:**

In newer construction, this doesn't seem to be much of an issue because the room is well vented for the boiler and any machinery located in it; however, in older homes this is not the case. You need to find out what the temperature will be in the boiler room during the winter months and what other equipment will be using the same space and if it will obstruct the air circulation.

4. **Garages:**

Most have poor air circulation, stagnant air, extreme temperatures, and odors. New construction garages are climate controlled and would be a candidate for venting.

5. **Carports:**

Carports provide a minimal amount of protection. You are still virtually venting to the outside. Although it is protected from the rain it is still subject to the extreme temperatures. Venting to an area like this has one advantage over some of the others in that there is a certain amount of natural air flow outside that helps if there is nowhere else to vent.

6. **Stairwells:**

Generally stagnant, noisy, hot exhaust and unsightly grill. Unit will draw in own exhaust.

7. **Air shafts/elevator/light shafts:**

Poor circulation; exhaust builds up extreme temperatures.

8. **Hallways:**

Again poor circulation; exhaust generally hangs around cooling unit to be sucked back in. Also noise, heat, and unsightly an grill on the outside of the cooling unit, facing into your living area.

9. **Living areas:**

Generally work well, but there are much better solutions than to vent to these areas. You have worked hard to get where you are today, and you have a beautiful home. Why screw it up with grills, noise, and excess heat? It doesn't make sense to me. It would be like having a window air conditioner in every room of your beautiful home instead of central air. You aren't gaining or saving anything.

10. Bathrooms/laundry rooms:

Generally too small and at times too warm from hot air exhaust buildup. Again, you own a beautiful home, so why screw it up with grills, noise, and excess heat?

11. Into interior spaces:

Although venting into a smaller space that opens up into a large more appropriate one sounds like it will work, it won't. The hot air exhaust will never find its way to the larger area because the cooling units generally use low 50 cfm (low rpms) and cannot blow the area more than ten or maybe twelve inches. The smaller area will create a tunneling effect and draw back in its own exhaust to cool itself, causing the cooling unit not to be able to keep temperature in the wine cellar.

Where, then, is there an appropriate place to vent for a through-the-wall unit? This can be answered in a one-on-one situation. Every wine cellar is unique, and so is the cooling system.

There are a lot of good places for wine cellars to be installed. They can go just about anywhere in the house or even garage if you take the proper precautions. The following places are examples of where people wanted to have a wine cellar but didn't want to go through everything to make it a proper wine cellar. When looking at these pictures, just remember that there are people who will tell you it will work just fine.

A closet off the bedroom

A crawl space

A damp basement

All of these places could be very good, if they are insulated and there is a vapor barrier with a proper cooling unit. In other words, if they are a "climate-controlled room". Just because a room is chilled for a while, that doesn't make it a wine cellar. The temperature and humidity must be maintained.

Let's talk a little bit about what to do and not to do to achieve that perfect wine cellar.

There are quite a few people who have a tape measure somewhere in their toolbox or in the kitchen drawer or even hanging on their key chain. I have found over a number of years in dealing with the customers, builders, contractors, and architects that some of these people do not have a clue what the numbers on the tape measure mean.

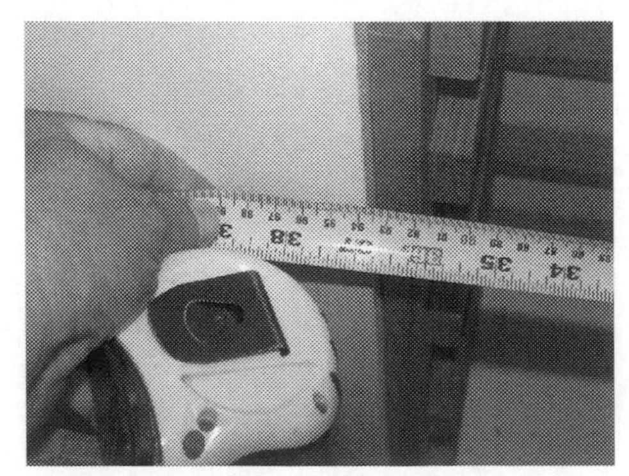

Good fit? Maybe not!

As you see from the picture, this looks like a great fit. The problem was that the wall measured thirty-seven inches and the racking came in at thirty-eight inches. This is the dilemma that always faces me when measurements are not taken correctly. When you get ready to measure your wall for your new wine cellar, don't just take somebody else's word for it. Get in there and take measurements on the bottom of the wall, in the middle of the wall, and also at the top of the wall. That way you can get an accurate measurement.

New construction

Now I know some of you are thinking that my walls aren't even up yet, or the studs aren't there, so why can't I just add an inch for drywall and be done with it? Again, the manufacturer that builds the racks for your new wine cellar can only build to the exact measurements you provide. They don't second-guess how thick the mud is or how thick the stone will be. Don't make your wine cellar builder who will install your racking do all kinds of other work that you may be charged for. Sometimes it is a lot cheaper to take the extra time and "measure twice."

Very close quarters

The wine cellar pictured here had some measurements that were off. The racking at the rear of the cellar was off by a good inch. I had everyone around me the whole time I was building this wine cellar. There was one comment made to me about the spacing being off a little bit. I simply told them that the measurements were off on the walls. The racking was built to the exact measurements given. I had to recut some of the racking but did not sacrifice any bottle count. This wine cellar had a bottle count of seven hundred-plus in a very small space.

After you get the most accurate measurements you can take, then it will be time to take those numbers to get a proper cooling unit. Here are some things to remember that go along with proper measurements.

Things that you must consider for the protection of your wine:

1. Constant temperature
2. Adequate humidity
3. Absence of strong light
4. Absence of any vibration

Calculate the Room Volume

Measure the height, width, and depth of your room and multiply each measurement to determine the cubic footage of wine cellar. If the room is not a rectangle, you will need to use geometry for your calculations. If your calculation results are between two sizes, always round up to the larger unit size. As a general rule, always overestimate rather than underestimate capacity.

Differentiate Between Inside/Outside Walls and Glass Doors/Windows

When figuring the calculations of your cellar space, it is important to take notice of the surrounding walls, floors, and ceiling. You might want to do a simple sketch just to understand what's around your new wine cellar.

- First, you will need to note whether walls are inside walls or outside walls.
- Second, you will need to see whether any walls have direct exposure to sunlight.
- Third, you will want to specify whether there is any glass (which should be insulated glass) in the door or windows on interior or exterior walls.

Calculate Heat Load

(Unit Size = Room Volume + Heat Load)

Heat load calculations provide information about the amount of heat introduced into the wine cellar by infiltration through the walls, the wine, the frequency of entry, mechanical sources (like lights) and humans. All this information will determine the heat load. If you have no glass and you insulate and weather strip your room properly, your heat load will equal zero. If you have glass and/or less than adequate insulation or are in a very hot climate, you need to increase the unit size (BTUH) to compensate.

Insulate, Weather Stripping, Glass

Inside walls and floors need a minimum of R11 insulation. Outside walls need a minimum or R19 (R30 with direct sunlight). An inside ceiling needs a minimum of R19 insulation (outside ceiling R30). Place the vapor barriers on the *hot* side of the insulation. Doors need to be exterior grade, and if there is glass in the door, it must be double-pane insulated glass.

If the wine cellar is located in a hot climate, round up to the next R-value. Always overestimate; never underestimate. Windows and doors need to be tightly sealed with weather stripping to prevent air leakage. Check under the door to make sure no air is leaking from seal outlets, switches, pipes, vents, and other possible air-leakage areas.

Here are some more tips that you will find in my column at CelebrityWineReview.TV/news.

Now we have covered a few of the questions that you should ask yourself. Building a wine a wine cellar is not like building a kitchen or a bathroom. It's time to ask some questions of the person whom you will hire to build your new wine cellar. So be prepared when your contractor gives you a few funny looks as you ask these questions.

First you need to ask the most important question:

How many climate-controlled wine rooms have you built?

If the answer here is, "Well I did this room one time that . . ." that's not a good answer! You want someone who has had experience with everything involved with a climate-controlled room. It is one thing to add on a room or remodel a kitchen, but when it comes to wine cellars, you need someone who really knows.

The second question you want to ask is about the materials to be used:

What are you going to use for materials?

What material will you use for the vapor and moisture barriers? How is this installed? The product used for this is one of the most important keys to building your new wine cellar. If you install it wrong or someone forgets to install it, you might as well not have a wine cellar.

The third question concerns the vapor barrier:

Are you sure you know why the vapor barrier is important? And do you know what could happen if it is not installed correctly?

Your average contractor may not know the answer. If they don't know the reasons behind the vapor barrier, at this point just say thanks and call an expert!

The fourth question you should have concerns the refrigeration equipment that will be installed:

How much noise will the cooling unit make, and where does it exhaust the hot air?

Some of the self-contained units are noisy and usually exhaust hot air into the adjacent room. Ask if they plan to use a split system? If they try to convince you that it doesn't matter, again just say thank you and call an expert.

Question number five covers repairs and replacements:

What would happen in the event that my cooling unit went on the fritz?

If you have to return it to the factory, with any luck you will have a replacement unit quickly. Or can the cooling unit be repaired locally? If not, your wine cellar could heat up rather quickly. Your wine is not going to like this.

The sixth question concerns the cooling unit and humidity:

Does the cooling unit that you are using have the capacity to increase the humidity without any additional equipment?

This is kind of a trick question. Most cooling units do not increase humidity unless you add a humidifier. They simply take out some humidity. If you find you need more humidity, a simple mister might do the trick.

Question number seven covers insurance:

Does your contractors' insurance cover the repairs if mold develops?

This goes hand and hand with the third question. If you develop mold or mildew, it could be because the wine cellar was not built right; the contractor should have insurance to cover this. Now it is not only your wine at risk; developing mold is very serious.

Question number eight is about the wine racks:

Where are the wine racks coming from?

Is the contractor building them, or are they coming from a manufacturer? Not that you are asking this to check up on them. The idea behind the question is just to know where your racks are coming from; you don't any want surprises. You want to know that your wine bottles are safely cradled in the racks. You don't want to find them lying on the floor one day.

Question number nine concerns the doors:

What kind of door are you installing?

If your contractor says, "We will match the doors here in the lower level; they are just hollow core doors anyway," that's the wrong answer. You need an insulated door with weather stripping all around. You can have glass in the door as long as it is insulated glass.

The last question concerns your bottles:

This question may sound a little funny. Do you know the weight of a bottle of wine?

Told you it sounds funny. But you are asking them to build racks for your wines, so think about it. You are asking them to construct a room that will only house one thing . . . *your wines!*

When you ask these questions of someone whom you will trust with your wines, make sure you get answers that are correct, not just something made up to sound good. If they get defensive through this questionnaire, again just say thank you and call an expert. It is not necessarily a bad thing if they admit to the lack of knowledge as long as they call in an expert.

Thanks, and may all your wines be great!

Next time let's talk about some great racks!

John Seitz

I will never forget building a wine cellar in Bakersfield, California. It was one of the most unusual wine cellars so far. The opening to the wine cellar was off the bar, where a giant wine barrel opened to a stairwell leading down into the wine cellar.

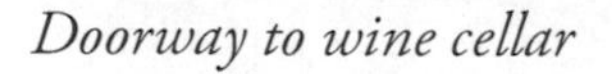

Doorway to wine cellar

Spiral stairway in the cellar

Before you even got to the wine cellar there was a jungle in his living room. In fact, when I was building his wine cellar the owner was in Montana shooting bears. He told me that he shot a ten-foot-tall black bear. Can you imagine a bear that big coming at you? My concern would be that the rifle would jam. Hopefully you have a backup just in case. The owner traveled around the world to go big-game hunting. Here are a couple of pictures from his living room.

This is something that would scare you in the middle of the night

Do I see an alligator in a tree?

What is for lunch today? And what wine will I have with it?

The time that I had picked to do a wine cellar job in Chicago was not the best time to be there. Later it would bring back memories of my first job. While I was there the snow and ice came in, and everyone said that it was too early for all this cold weather to be here. I parked The Wine Cellar RV at a Costco parking lot that was about five miles from the jobsite. You see, in the wintertime all the RV parks in the north are closed. I never thought I would be there in the winter.

This wine cellar that I was building should have taken only three days max, but it turned into a ten-day project. This wine cellar had stops and starts all over the room. The cabinets had to be custom made on the jobsite. It was something that I did not think was going to happen.

The nights were brutal, with winds howling at about forty miles an hour. I had a heater in the bay of the RV, where the water lines were, so they would not freeze up. I did not want to go through the things that I went through before with the other RV. My generator ran almost twenty-four hours a day. Since the job was lasting longer than I had figured, other things would come into play. I was running out of fresh water. My customer had found a gas station that let me fill up my water tanks. Now I had fresh water, but the other thing to be concerned about was the usage of it. I had a 150-gallon tank of fresh water and a 170-gallon tank for the waste water to go to. Not a problem right? Well, the other water from the previous fresh water was already drained into the waste tanks. These are all things that you find out about when you get out on the road. When I finally finished up the wine cellar on a Saturday I was ready to leave the cold.

Custom racking for a round room

The customer asked me if I would join them for dinner at the country club. My response was yes, not thinking that I didn't have any clothes to wear to a country club—good thing Costco was still open. When we came back from dinner, my thoughts were about departing for a warmer climate in the morning.

So is it just me, or do all people have this much trouble with RVs? When I woke up the next morning, my refrigerator wasn't working. I went to the first RV shop I could find, and they checked out everything and found out I needed a new refrigerator. This would be the first of three refrigerators I would have to obtain. Buying a refrigerator for an RV is not like going to your local store and picking one out. These are special refrigerators, and there are only a few places in the country that make them. This would be the first of many adaventures that I will encounter with refrigerators in the future.

It took about three weeks for me to get one ordered and delivered to a RV shop in Mississippi. The first refrigerator came in, and of course it didn't work, so I had to wait for another one. When the new one got there, it took all day for the service department to install it. The side window of the RV had to come out in order for them to swap the refrigerators. Finally I had a new refrigerator and I could buy food again. Life was good—until the next dilemma.

My next wine cellar job would take me back to southern California again, where I would find out that the customer had left the cork floor out in weather. It was only partially wrapped in plastic and was not supposed to be outside. Everything buckled, and I had to postpone the job until they purchased a new floor. I went back to New York to do my next job and then traveled back across the country to California a few weeks later to do this job. I am so glad that fuel prices were not as high then as they are now.

Stained redwood with a polyurethane finish

This was an unusual wine cellar where you would go down a flight of stairs and go into a bar area. The left side of the bar was racks for wine. The racks would slide and you would enter the wine cellar. The ceiling was curved.

Sometimes very funny things happened to me when traveling back and forth across the country. I was going through a toll booth in Oklahoma when a lady in the middle booth yelled over at me and asked if I was John Seitz. She had a magazine with my picture in it and wanted to get my autograph. She said that she had seen me come through before and just waited till I came back again. I pulled over to sign her magazine and gave her a bottle of wine. This Corvette that was behind me followed me into the fuel stop in Joplin, Missouri, a few miles down the road. He asked me if I was famous (obviously he didn't drink wine). I gave him a copy of the magazine and autographed it for him. We talked about wine and wine cellars for a little while. He had only drank wine a time or two and was not into it.

There are some times when it takes longer to set up for the job than the job actually takes. For one job in northern Illinois, that was the case. It had been raining all night and into the morning when I arrived at the job. I was shown where the job was, and I proceeded to go to work. I was amazed at the wine racks that had been installed a few years earlier by someone else. Before doing anything, I had to make sure that what I had to do would not hinder the rest of the racking. Since the racks were full of wine, nailing would be a little difficult. I secured everything around the stemware rack that was to be replaced. Then, finally pulling out the rack and feeling confident that I could remove it, I was just about ready to replace it with an arch. After installing the arch, I asked the customer why they were taking out the stemware rack. She said that her husband just wanted to. Now it was time to take all my tools back out to the RV and get to the next job.

Before, with the stemware rack After, with the arch installed

Some of the cool things I wound up doing as The Master Wine Cellar Builder, had to do with some of the shows that I do. In Washington, DC, I wound up with ten cases of wine from some of the exhibitors. They didn't want to haul it back with them, so they just gave me some of the wines. Of course during the show I would go around to taste some of the wines they had. And just like at the wineries and vineyards I visited, all I had to say was that I liked that wine and they would give me a bottle or two. Someone has to live this rough life I lead.

Wine tasting in Washington, DC

Show in Baltimore

When I stopped in an RV park in South Carolina one night, I was not feeling very well. I started to get a headache and a little chest pain. Sometimes you just don't think about a heart attack. I took a couple of Bufferin pills, had dinner, and went to bed. I felt a lot better the next day. I had a big breakfast, did laundry, and even walked around the park. Life was pretty good. After getting everything together, I was on my way to New York again. I left the RV park and started down the highway. It wasn't very long before that feeling from the night before came back. I quickly punched in hospital in my GPS. The nearest was about three miles away. I plugged in a course for it, and off I went. Looking back on this adventure I suppose I should have called an ambulance instead. But I also had The Wine Cellar RV to think about.

Pulling into the parking lot was almost more than I could take. I walked across the parking lot and asked the attendant where the emergency room was. He looked at me and said, "Let me help you." Once inside the emergency room, I told the nurse I thought I was having a heart attack. I didn't even get all the words out before they stuck me in a wheelchair and raced off to the emergency room. Everybody was standing around taking my blood pressure and also my blood. They had given me some nitroglycerin to slow my heart down. After what seemed like an eternity, I was rolled up into my room for the night hooked up to a bunch of wires. I was woken up several times the first night by nurses taking my blood and blood pressure and giving me pills to put me back to sleep.

The next day was very rigorous. They started off by rolling me into a CAT scan contraption. Next were scans up and down the main arteries in my body. Then finally, after being poked and prodded all day, I was rolled back in my room. I missed lunch and did not get to put my order in for dinner either. I know they do what they think is best for you under these conditions. Now maybe I could relax a little bit after a grueling day. About an hour had passed when they came to get me again for more tests, taking blood, prodding me like cattle, and going through all kinds of x-rays. *This is for all the best*, I kept telling myself. They even did a scope through my heart to see if there were any blockages. Four days later, the heart doctor came in and told me that I did not have a heart attack. So that was good news, right? That was not the end of it; he said the specialist would be in to talk to me about the rest. That was a long couple of minutes of my life. The specialist told me that what I had was a stroke. I did not know what to say to all this. My perception of a stroke was that you would be paralyzed in one way or another. Before I left I was on a regimen of pills from morning to night. This is not a thing that I wanted to do the rest of my life.

All the time I was in the hospital, I never gave a second thought to The Wine Cellar RV being parked in the parking lot. Getting back in there and driving it was a little scary. Pretty soon I was back on the road and headed to New York for my next wine cellar. The good thing about all this was that about two years later I would be taken off all medication.

I went back to New York and waited for my next job. In the meantime I received a call from a company in California asking me to talk with them about building wine cellars for their customers. I flew to San Diego to discuss building wine cellars for them. That seemed like a good idea at the time and proved to be good later down the road. I had a chance while in Los Angeles California to talk with another wine cellar company. They said I would be advertised on their website. When I got back to New York, the deal with the first company seemed to have gone south. The partner of the man I had spoken with wasn't exactly thrilled about the situation. We were supposed to have the final phone conversation to close the deal. He didn't bother to call me when he said he would. I e-mailed him several times, and he did not respond. Finally I told him that if this was the way he ran his business, I didn't want any part of it. It was really funny that he e-mailed me back a few days later telling me that would not do business with me at all. That company went out of business a few years later. The original owner of the company tried to revive the company a few months later, but not with the same partner. Now they have a great company and are thriving. They have a great craftsman who sculpts some of their woodwork. He is the fourth generation of this craft handed down through the carpenters in his family.

Next I took a trip to New Hampshire to talk to the manufacturer, Vigilant Wine Cellars, about consulting and building wine cellars for their clients. The meeting went quite well, I thought. One of the owners gave me a tour of the plant. Employees had their own stations to work at performing different parts of the assembly of the cellars. The cabinet shop was quite impressive. We went to lunch, and I left to go back to work thinking that I would do wine cellars for them. But I never did a wine cellar for them directly. Looking back on this now, I guess that was just a waste of time for me.

My next job would take me across the country again. I will soon find myself constructing a cellar at another Ruth's Chris Steakhouse, this one in Mishawaka, Indiana. They called it the Regis Room, and it took about four days to build. The windows in the room were the most challenging part. The racks were so close that there was no room for error. This would be my third wine room built for Ruth's Chris Steakhouse. The carpenters were still on the job, and everyone kept coming in my wine room to see what I was doing

Ruth's Chris Steakhouse in Mishawaka, Indiana

As I traveled around the country, I would be at a lot of benefits for a lot of different charities and great causes. This one was for the Breast Cancer Foundation. I had a chance to meet the firemen who drove The Pink Fire Truck from coast to coast.

The Pink Fire Truck with Pink Ribbon Tour

I was invited to do a show in Las Vegas Nevada, at the Homebuilders Convention. I took both of my daughters with me on this trip. We flew out there and now I know why driving around in The Wine Cellar RV is better. We all had a good time seeing the town. My daughters went around the city doing the tourist thing. I wish I could have been with them to show off some of the city. My daughters did the thing they do best on vacation—they slept till noon. I had a show to do, so I was up at six in the morning to get ready. They tried their luck at the big machines. Needless to say, they did not win.

Daughter Mary Lauren

Daughter Colleen

During the middle of the week, I flew to Salt Lake City Utah, to try to secure another contract to build wine cellars for Wine Racks America, and built a wine cellar for one of their clients about six months later.

When we got back to my home in St. Louis from Las Vegas, there was a flyer on the door from the city of St. Charles. It was from the inspector's office telling me that I could not park The Wine Cellar RV at my house anymore. The only reason I had bought the house was because I could park my motor home here. There were other motor homes in the neighborhood also. Maybe he did not like wine, or he just drank beer! They were going to fine me $1,000 a day if I did not move it. I tried to talk with the inspector, but he never returned any of my calls. Finally, when I knew my house was sold, I just figured he would go away. The last day I was there he took a picture of The Wine Cellar RV in front of the house and tried to get me into court. I went to his boss and told him that I sold the house and no longer lived there. He told me not to worry about it and he would take care of it. My house was sold pretty fast with the help of my friend John Vasel, my real estate agent.

I would be on my way to Florida soon and not have to worry about him anymore. Everything was moved out of the house, and I was now officially "homeless". I was on my way to Florida to build a wine cellar for a company out of Orlando. When I got there, I found out that the wine cellar was not ready for me yet, this was no surprise to me. The wine cellar belonged to Annika Sorenstam (LPG Pro). The contractor still had walls to finish and also stonework. I stayed at an RV resort about twenty miles from the jobsite. The bad thing about staying there was that it rained all week. I didn't get a chance to enjoy the amenities of the resort—the pools, the hot tubs, or anything else they had. One day when I was sitting inside the motor home watching TV, I noticed that there was water running on the floor. My first thought was that I had a leak in the roof, but when I got up I realized that the commode was running over (with clean water). The handle had gotten stuck and overflowed. I started to clean up all the mess, noticing that water had now made its way under the floor. The new wood floor that I had just installed a couple of months before was now warping. Luckily the sub-floor was still in good shape. After getting everything dried out, I had to think about getting a new floor.

Putting in a new floor in the RV

The wine cellar in Orlando was now ready for me to install. I spent about three days on the job itself. I liked what the contractor had done with the stonework. The wine racks were a dark stain. Not a big wine cellar, but a unique one.

Check out the stone work

My next adventure would take me to Virginia. I had lots of time to get there, so I went the southern route through Mississippi and Alabama. When I started this job, I did as I always do, I laid out the material. I found out that all the parts weren't there. So I built what I could, ordered the rest of the material, and went to see some friends for a while. This wine cellar was for the man who ran the air force. The wine cellar had a dark stain and would house about eight hundred bottles. It would have been a simple job to do, if I had all the parts.

I went to Richmond, Virginia, for a couple of days to see some friends. On the way back to my jobsite, I decided to take a back road, and I am glad I did. My steering box fell out a half mile from a repair shop. I managed to pull the RV in there. As they inspected it they asked me how I had managed to steer it in there. Somebody was sure looking out for me that day. This was fixed a couple days later. There is never a dull moment, but that's the way of life in an RV—sometimes good, sometimes bad.

I started the wine cellar job again in Virginia with all the parts on hand, figuring I had a couple more days with the job. A United Van Line driver asked me to move out of his way in a cul-de-sac. After looking on the side on my vehicle, he said that he had some wines given to him by one of his customers and asked me if I could tell him little about the wines. I had looked at the wines he had but told him that these wines wouldn't last in his trailer. The trailer could heat up to 110 degrees. That would definitely ruin them. One of the wines was a Rothschild 95 Lafite. The driver asked me if I wanted it, not knowing what he had. I did take it after explaining to him what this bottle of wine might be worth. He told me to take it anyway.

That evening, after I finished the wine cellar, my customer asked me to stay for dinner and share some wine in appreciation for the job, I did. During dinner I told the story of this bottle of wine I had received from the driver with United Van Lines. He seemed puzzled that someone would give away an expensive bottle of wine like that. I knew that the bottle of wine really would not do me any good, since I was not going to drink it anyway. I told him I would give it to him since he appreciated good wines. They asked me to autograph it as they would put the wine in place of honor so everyone could see it.

Designer kits with a dark stain

My next wine cellar would be built at the Ruth's Chris Steakhouse in St. Louis at the Hyatt hotel. My friend John Vasel helped me with this one. This also had to be done at night again, because of union rules. I started this job on a Friday night and finished up on Sunday. There were lockers for the customers to store their private wine in. A lot of places were doing this to keep customers' favorite wines on hand.

Ruth's Chris at the start Ruth's Chris three days later

After this job I had a little time on my hands and decided to go southwest. I stayed at the Downstream Casino where they had free hookups for RV. This casino was located right on the border of Missouri and Oklahoma. This is where I saw a Credence Clearwater concert. The casino gave me backstage passes for myself and a few people I met at the park. This is one of the benefits of being The Master Wine Cellar Builder. This is one of those places that you look for when traveling down the road. The water and electric were free of charge. Of course, when you went into the casino, you paid for it if you lost.

The manufacturer I talked about earlier in Utah sent me the paperwork to build a wine cellar outside of Salt Lake City Ut. The customer had about a seven-hundred-bottle wine cellar. Since this was my first wine cellar for this company, I noticed that there were a couple of things they did that were different from the things done by other companies. The curved corners were put together differently than most. To make things even more difficult, the company didn't send me the parts needed to install the curved corner. I had to drive back to the manufacturer to discuss this and get the rest of the material.

When I got back to the manufacturer, they told me that they had just forgotten to send the pieces out. After I saw the missing pieces, it all made sense. When I was done with this wine cellar, the customer invited me upstairs for a toast to their new cellar. They wrote to the company about my work:

> Maurice from Salt Lake City said:
> August 21st, 2009 at 1:33:58 PM
> John is downstairs building our 600+ wine cellar as I write this. A consummate professional, raconteur, and all-around great guy!

While traveling around the country is very interesting, you just might see some interesting vehicles right at home. This was a peanut mobile passing through town.

A giant Peanut Car

Some of the things that you run into around the country are really unique, like the view from twenty-two floors above the ocean in West Palm Beach, Florida, to having a nine-hole golf course right on the property, at a luxury RV resort. Things are always interesting for a guy like me.

A great resort to stay in

Sometimes I have the opportunity to let a lot of people enjoy some of the great wines that I always take for granted. This was the case at a golf and rv resort, Torrey Oaks Golf and RV Resorts. I stayed in for a few months one winter. I had a free pass for three days there, and it turned out to be three months before I left. The golf course was right next door, and all I had to do was jump in my golf cart, so I played golf almost every day. Someone would always ask me to play. This is also where I would meet my new best friend, Torrey. In February, a man came into the park one day with a dog that had wound up at his doorstep. He was looking for the owner at all the RV parks in the area. This dog jumped out of his truck and came straight to me. The man asked me if this was my dog, because he seemed to know me. My dog Buster had died a couple of years earlier, and I didn't want another dog. The man came back a couple of weeks later and still had this dog. He said that he would have to put him in the dog pound since he hadn't found the owner yet. He asked me if I would take him because he came to me again. When I found out that the dog pound only kept them for twenty-four hours, I called the man and told him to bring me the dog.

Torrey was a good dog from the very beginning. He was an English Springer, and I think someone had worked with him before. It was a few months before Torrey even barked. Now he thinks he owns the RV and pretty well does what he wants to.

Wine Tasting

My new best friend, Torrey

When I got back to St. Louis, my kids and everyone else who met Torrey thought he was just the best dog. My daughter's dog thought that she had a new playmate. They were in the backyard running around and having a good time when Molly, my daughter's dog, came to the back door by herself. I looked for Torrey, and he was nowhere to be found. He had jumped a four-foot fence and was at the neighbor's house just browsing. We all had a good laugh about it, but he is definitely not street smart. I do keep him on a leach.

I never thought I would be told that The Wine Cellar RV would not be allowed somewhere until I had a wine cellar job to do in Hilton Head North Carolina. I found out that I couldn't drive the RV to the property because there were some laws not permitting RVs or motorcycles on the island. But yet they allowed old trucks and cars that emitted smoke and oil onto the island. I wound up staying at a very posh RV resort. The park was very nice, with all the amenities, but also was very expensive. The customer said he would pay for it. I gave him a bill twice, then finally paid me.

While there I did see one thing that kept an eye on a lot of things. This Hawk high above where I had The Wine Cellar RV parked, kept looking down at me. Did he think I was his dinner or was he just looking?

Hawk perched on a tree limb

The wine cellar that I built for this customer was made of oak. This particular wine cellar had door openings on three sides of it. One set of doors opened to the deck, the other doors opened to the hallway. Then of course one door was the main door to get into the wine cellar. The design of wine racks had to cover one of the doors coming in from a hallway. Not a choice I certainly would make. I am sure it had something to do with the laws of the condo.

See the door behind the diamond bin on the left?

I finished this job up in about a week and was on my way to my next wine cellar adventure.

When I was leaving a customer's house in the southeast one time, I had a previous customers call and tell me that his basement had flooded. His summer home was in the Hamptons on Long Island, and now he may need a new wine cellar. I told him I would try to save as much as possible. When I arrived at the jobsite, it was a mess. The wood was now stained from all the water in the basement. He not only had the wine cellar ruined, but he sustained heavy damage throughout the living area. After moving a few hundred bottles of wine, I now had the challenge to save as much of the wine cellar as possible. It took me only a day to tear it apart, and I managed to save about one-third of it. It would be several weeks before I would get back there to install the new wine cellar.

When I built the wine cellar for Regis Philbin, I couldn't get The Wine Cellar RV down his street either. I would have to rent a vehicle to do his job. Regis and Joy Philbin were very nice people to work for. They were down to earth and not what you would expect from a big star like that. Joy would make breakfast for Regis. I would have thought they would have a cook who would do all that. This job was supposed to be a weekend job only. Wouldn't you know it; his job would be short of material, not just a piece, but a whole cabinet. I would have it shipped there and be back the following week. While I was at Regis's home, Joy asked me to replace a light bulb that had burned out in the kitchen. I had started to unscrew it when it popped and fused to the base. I jumped down from the counter pretty quickly so as not to get electrocuted. With Regis standing there watching me, I did not want to look too dumb. I kneeled on the counter and started to unscrew the bulb again. Well, this time the whole fixture came apart. I guess, looking back on that now, it was pretty funny. Finally I said, "You need to call your electrician." He showed up about an hour later and fixed it pretty quick. So this would answer that age old question: How many wine cellar builders does it take to change a light bulb? None! You call an electrician

I was interviewed by Fox2 News on September 3, 2010. Tim Ezzell did the interview with me for about three minutes. Just like all the rest of the interviews it seemed to take longer to get The Wine Cellar RV set up, than actual TV time. This was also where I made the announcement about being the wine cellar expert on Celebrity Wine Review TV.

Inside the Wine Cellar RV with Tim Ezzell

It seems like I am always trying to fix things in the RV. I recently tried to get a leak fixed in the bathroom. Not as bad as the leak before. When I got the part to fix it, wouldn't you know it was the wrong piece? A lot of times you try to save a few dollars by doing it yourself. Having the right part is always better. Of course having the know-how also helps. My friend John Vasel came over to take me to the parts store to get the right piece this time.

Now I Am headed off to my next wine cellar. While stopped at a rest area the middle of nowhere,Ohio, I was walking my dog, when a truck driver came up to me and said, "Didn't I just see you on TV in St. Louis?" It's nice when people recognize me all over the country. I told him I was just on TV. Asked him if he drank wine and his reply was a resounding yes. I gave him a bottle of wine, which he asked me to autograph.

Seems like everyone has a story out here. I met some very interesting people when I went to a campground in New Jersey to refresh water supplies in the RV. I met a couple with their three kids. He was an attorney who traveled around the country trying to find his niche. They had bought a 1997 American Eagle to live in full-time while traveling. On his first trip out a tractor-trailer backed into him while he was on an off-ramp. They said it did about $8,000 in damages. He said that he would be fighting the insurance company over this. So far he had to pay for all the out-of-pocket expenses himself. I asked him about his children. He said they would be homeschooled every other year. That way they will still make friends at their school; being on the road can provide children with quite an education. They can not only read about historic places but actually see them. I wished him well in all his endeavors. He was quite impressed to meet me. He said he never heard of A Master Wine Cellar Builder. I told him that not too many people outside the wine world have.

He told me that when he makes his fortune and buys that big house I could come over and build that wine cellar for him.

There are a couple of other interesting people that I met when I was in New Jersey. I went to the Wal-Mart Resort (in the parking lot of Wal-Mart). There I met a homeless and jobless man in a van. His only friend seemed to be his dog. I talked with him for a while, and he seemed to be very educated. He had lost his first wife and then made the fatal mistake of marrying again. His second wife was a gold digger, he told me. She managed to take him for all that he had. He wound up having a couple of heart attacks, which kept him from leaving the area. His goal was to wind up in Montana and live out his life on a farm. Sounds like something our parents told us about where the family dog went to when he got old. So for now he was living in his van. People gave him things: food for him, and an overwhelming amount of food for his dog. As I was speaking to him a man came up and said hello to the dog, put some water in the dog's bowl, and then gave the man some money. The guy had not asked for any money. When the generous man left he looked in his pocket. This man was just given a hundred dollars. Not bad, but I wouldn't want to be in his shoes. The guy was not looking for a handout; apparently people knew about him and just gave him things and money. He seemed to leave during the day and come back in the evening. He had a generator for electricity. He also told me about another man who lived on the parking lot.

The second man's story is also one of the economy. He had come up from Florida looking for work. He had said that the work in Florida was running out fast. If you wanted to work, you could find a job for maybe five or six dollars an hour. He found some work up here in the New Jersey area. He was a salesman selling for a construction company and thought things were going to get better for him. The company was going out of business as a result of misappropriation of funds. The guy said that he was stealing from his own company, so he had to go look elsewhere. He tried to find some work at other places, but there didn't seem to be anything else available at the time. He went to Applebee's with a friend and had a couple of beers. On his way back home he was stopped by the police. Yeah, you guessed it. He was over the blood alcohol level and was hauled off to jail. Not that that was enough, but he had also just lost his insurance on his vehicle. In New Jersey, it's a felony to drive without insurance. Now this guy faced felony charges along with being over the alcohol limit. He was in jail for a while, and the place where he was staying also kicked him out for nonpayment of rent. There was not a whole lot he could do at this time. He got his insurance reinstated, but the sad thing about all this was that his insurance would be up the day he went to court. Life just doesn't seem fair sometimes. He told me that not only was all this going on, but his truck payment was four months overdue as well. Now they would repossess his vehicle also. The guy had two little dogs that stay with him for company. When I made dinner that night, I asked him to join me, not out of pity, but out of compassion. He said that this sure does beat a bag of potato chips. If they came to get his truck, maybe he could live with the other guy in the van.

It just seems that there are more and more of these stories around the country. You see people aimlessly walking the streets. The economy has hit a lot of people really hard. I don't know what will happen to these guys, but I wish them well.

Life on the road just simply amazes me sometimes. One time, as I sat in New Jersey waiting to install the next wine cellar, I had to pull into an RV park to take on some fresh water and obviously dump the old water. I met some people in there who were on their first RV journey. They were in a small pull-behind trailer. As they started to get set up with electricity, water, and sewer, the owner realized that he didn't have a sewer hose or water hose in this trailer. They had just bought this camper and come from the dealer. He called the people from whom he had purchased the camper, and they told him that he had to buy that stuff. I told him that those things usually come with the RV. He did not seem to know that these RV salespeople don't tell you all the things you need to know. I told him that I had been in the same place with my first RV and had done that. I was surprised, though, that they did not get at least a dumping hose, which is standard equipment. He went out and bought the things he needed and started to set up again.

Funny thing about drain hoses—sometimes they just are not long enough. His trailer was unhooked and leveled already, so he wasn't going to move it again. I knew it wasn't right, but I just kind of chuckled to myself and figured that everyone had to learn. I helped him as much as I could. Later they invited me over for a drink, and we all talked and laughed about the future of RVing. Little did I know that my fate was going to be challenged later that evening.

I was looking for a snack in my refrigerator and thought to myself that it really wasn't as cold as it had been a few hours before. But of course this refrigerator was only a couple of years old, so there wasn't any concern. When I went to bed that night, I never gave it a second thought. In the morning it all hit the fan. The refrigerator temperature was now at around forty-eight degrees. I had just spent $4,000 a couple of years ago to get a new one. Then six months ago the cooling unit went out. I wound up waiting for the part for about a week and a half. Now it appeared that I was having the same troubles again. How could this be happening all over again?

I called Dometic, the company that makes the refrigerator, and told them of my problems. They were very attentive but said that I needed to go to service dealer and let them diagnose the problem. That was great except for one thing: I had a job to do the next day and no one could get to me before the following week. There was one problem after another, and finally after I waited on hold for an hour and ten minutes they said that if I could get someone to verify that the cooling unit was broken, they would send a new unit to where I would be. This would prove to be another problem all by itself. Now I just needed to find that service person at an RV dealer.

After several phone calls, I found a dealer who told me to leave it off overnight and it might fix itself. *Was he kidding me?* So now I was back just waiting till the next day, when just maybe I could get my wine cellar installed in New Jersey. Things did not get better with the refrigerator since the cooling coil was broken.

Maybe on the bright side of things, my next job in North Carolina had the racking delivered early. But next I received an e-mail that there were broken pieces in the boxes. Not only would that stop me from doing my job, but it would also push things out further. The e-mails are now going back and forth between the factory, the customer, my client, and me. Life just kept getting better.

I finally got a hold of Mark in the Dometic warranty department and told him I did not want this fixed again. I wanted a new refrigerator for the RV. He said that he would give me a new refrigerator, and that was great news. The downside was that there had to be a little remodeling done. The new refrigerator was taller and deeper, which was great as far as I was concerned. Now I had to find someone to do it. I wondered whether the factory would accept it if I cut out the space. I would find out the following week. I would be without a refrigerator for about one month.

I was now ready to start on my job in Sag Harbor the following Monday. Since I had already put this wine cellar together once, it should go pretty quickly the second time. I got there, and the carpenters were still not quite ready for me. I just stood around for a couple of hours before I could start. I worked late into the night, and at the end of the first day, I was halfway through the job. The next day I started early and again worked late to get the job almost finished. I was set to be done by noon on Wednesday, and I would have beaten my old record. This was a four-thousand-bottle wine cellar, and I ended up taking two and half days total, a new record.

I planned to head toward Highlands, North Carolina, on Wednesday afternoon and hopefully meet the customer on Sunday at his house. The next-door neighbor in Sag Harbor came over before I left. He said he was inviting me over for dinner that night. I thought that was nice of him. I was thinking along the lines of a glass of wine. I said to him, "Do you like to drink great wines?" He said yes, and my response was "Then invite me over for that."

On my way North Carolina, I looked around for an RV park near my next stop. I came across a park about twenty miles from where I needed to be. I talked with the owner, and he told me to get there as fast as I could, because they were having Oktoberfest and I would enjoy it. The park was at Lake Toxaway. I arrived there on Friday, but the owner was not there. One of the other people showed me to my site. I got all squared away and was walking my dog when the owner showed up. We went to the office for registration. I gave him my credit card, and he looked at me and said, "We accept only cash." That was a big shock, since he hadn't said anything when I spoke with him before. I asked him if there was an ATM around, and he said, "No." I asked him if someone could take me to get some cash. He said, "Well, I guess you can't stay here." Needless to say I was upset and didn't know where to go at that point.

I started toward the town of Highlands. The mountains were no place I wanted to be at night. Daylight was bad enough to be driving down hills and around hairpin curves. I soon found some of those hairpin curves. I kept gearing down till I was in first gear and going about ten miles an hour. I know the people behind were not happy. Finally I found another RV park. The cost didn't matter at that point. They had all the things you look for, including hot tubs, a workout room, and swimming pools. I stayed there over the weekend and met some nice people with whom I shared some wine and conversation.

On Sunday I left to go back up the mountain and to the golf course where my next wine cellar would be. I went down one road and made a wrong turn. The road made a hairpin turn that I couldn't get around. I had to either back down, not my first choice, or turn around. As I started the turn around, I could only go back and forth about an inch. It took about a half an hour to get through this. At one point I thought that I would turn the bus over, but I finally went the right way and wound up at the customer's house.

This wine cellar would hold about two thousand bottles, and I figured it would take about three days. Two days later I was on my way. The customer gave me six bottles of wine to get me going. These are some of the benefits of being the master wine cellar builder.

During the time I spent in Highlands, North Carolina, I saw beautiful homes nestled around a great golf course. I built a custom wine cellar for an attorney and his wife. They used this place on the golf course for their getaway. The scenery was breathtaking. The golf course was one that Tiger Woods would be proud to play on. It was only about a two-and-a-half-hour drive north of Atlanta, Georgia. As I said before, the roads to get there were very small and very, very, curvy. Trying to drive The Wine Cellar RV to the house was challenging, to say the least. As I drove toward the house, I made a wrong turn and thought I was going to turn the RV on its side. A little scary; if my dog had looked out the passenger's side of the bus, maybe I would have turned it over.

This particular wine cellar, just like many others, didn't go without a hitch. After nine changes were made, the final drawing was ready to be put into production. The customer stayed in contact with me so I could build this wine cellar when the time came. The factory was supposed to have all my material to the house by October 11. They delivered on time, but the carrier that delivered it had a slight complication, and four boxes were broken. The customer was fit to be tied, and when I heard this, I thought my job would be put off for a while. Luckily, Tony Wilke from the manufacturer, Wine Cellar Innovation, stepped in along with Dave Elliot and expedited the new material to the jobsite. Almost all of the material arrived the day before I was scheduled to arrive. The other box arrived one of the days while I was on the jobsite. Thank you very much,

Tony and Dave. I looked over everything when I arrived, and all was well again.

Redwood wine cellar

The wine cellar shown here is about 2,200 bottles. There is a lot of case storage under the individual racking. This particular wine cellar is all heart redwood. It will store Champagne, Bordeaux, magnums and jeroboams. This is at the front, under the table top. At the very front of the main cellar are racks for magnums; the rest are for 750 ml. As you can see there is a variety in this 2,200-bottle wine cellar. The client could buy more wine by the case to store for enjoyment at a later date.

Building wine cellars for people is the best "job" I have ever had. The look on someone's face when he or she sees the wine cellar is always remarkable to me. The comment is "Now it is actually here, not just on paper or a computer drawing." A number of my clients also say to me, "This is more than I ever expected." The wines that I have personally consumed when toasting the wine cellars are far beyond what I ever thought I would be drinking. I have to admit that I believe I have tasted some of the finest wines in the world. After a couple of long days working on this wine cellar, the finished product was very pleasing to my customer and of course to me.

Can't wait to put all my wine here!

Let me get to the next job and let's see what it will bring . . . Will it be smaller? Will it be larger? Tune in and find out.

Now I was finally on my way to St. Louis to get the refrigerator taken care of. I made some phone calls to Dometic and the RV dealer Apache Village RV in St. Louis. I made all the necessary arrangements to get the refrigerator swapped out. Hopefully I would have one again by Monday night. But of course, in the real world, that won't happen. This will be the third refrigerator in the RV.

During the day on Monday, I wrote another article for Celebrity Wine Cellar Review TV. I stayed in their waiting room all day, and toward the afternoon I knew the work would not be completed that day. Torrey and I had to check into a hotel down the street. When checking in, I got sticker shock. Since I do not normally stay at a hotel, the price of a room seemed a bit much to me. That night I couldn't get much sleep; the bed wasn't very comfortable, and my dog Torrey was up every time some walked by the door. They had a good breakfast that was complimentary, to offset the price of the room, I guess.

Taking my time to get back to the dealer, I hoped the work on the RV would be done by the time I returned. I knew by the look on the service manager's face that the refrigerator was not done yet. He told me that it would be a few hours yet. They did a great job cutting out for the new refrigerator. The only bad part was that I lost a drawer on the bottom of the cabinet and now the new refrigerator stuck into the hallway about three inches. I guess you have to make some concessions; after all, I now had a new refrigerator that was a lot bigger that before. When they brought the RV back to me, I noticed that after all that went on with conversations, pictures, and everything else, my new refrigerator did not have an ice maker, plus the front door had a dent in it. I called Mark at Dometic back and told him about the ice maker. He said that the refrigerator he had sent out was supposed to have one in it, along with a water dispenser in the door. I told him to just send a new door to replace the dented one and I would live without the ice maker.

Now Torrey and I were about to embark on our next adventure. I now just had to wait for the new refrigerator to cool down to buy food again. Torrey was happy to be back in his home again. He took a little nap right away when I stopped at the store. Life was good again for Torrey and me.

The trip out to California this time was an adventure you soon don't forget. Leaving St. Louis at the end of November provided a good opportunity to be headed toward a warmer climate. Traveling down Interstate 55 south seemed to be a good choice at the time. I stopped off at Fredericktown, Missouri, to visit some family for a while before heading out MO 67. I spent the night there, and the next day we fixed a couple of things on the RV and I traveled down toward Little Rock, Arkansas The roadway they are building is almost complete going through the Ozarks. I remember the up-and-down hills curving back and forth. The road seemed to never end. Now you can put your cruise control on and pretty well leave it alone for many miles to come. I spent a couple of days in an RV park that was along the river in Little Rock Arkansas. I had a nice view from my place, looking onto the river and the River Complex on the other side. There are little shops and restaurants. I found a great steak house and had dinner there that night. Everyone came up to me and wondered what I did for a living. A no-brainer there, look at the writing on the RV. I found a couple of people who were wine drinkers, and we opened up a fine bottle of Napa Cellars '07.

The next day I was on my way to Texarkana to get into a resort with a golf course. I was very excited and looked forward to spending some time in this place. That night I stopped in a little RV park on the border of Texas and Arkansas. Good price, and they had green grass for my dog (that would disappear later the farther west I went) and things that you would want for an overnight stay.

It was now Sunday morning, and I was on my way to the resort. Looking around the area, I saw nice scenery, a small river, and great roads. When I turned into the "resort area" it was a different story. My cell phone wasn't working anymore and this "resort" and the surroundings did not look very favorable, but I was trying to keep an open mind. I went to the guard shack to register. The guard told me they were "under renovation"; this was not a good sign. As I followed him to my RV site, the "lake" was nothing but a giant puddle with green stuff on top. The golf course was not maintained at all, but I figured I could stay here and just relax for a few days anyway. Once I pulled into the site, there was no way I could level my RV out to stay there. I asked the guard if there was another site he could put me on. Not that the place was full anyway. He said it was no problem, I could just pick where I wanted to stay. In the meantime I noticed that there was no phone reception on my cell phone here either. I asked him about the cable TV. He said they didn't have it. When I asked him about local TV stations, his reply was that it was too far out to get TV. Now we had a real problem. No golf, bad RV site, no TV, no computer, no phone. I was certainly not going to stay in a bad place for three days with nothing to do and have to listen to a salesman tell me what a great place this is. I told the guard that this was not a place for me and I was leaving. He told me I may have to pay a fee. Go ahead and collect it. You don't have a credit card on file, so what are you going to do? What was I going to do now? I had these days figured in my trip to California.When I left there, I was in a kind of stupor.

I called the company with whom I had made the arrangements. They told me that they were undergoing some construction and were sorry. They couldn't have said something before? Now was not the time to find out about all this. I did have in my plans to play golf and enjoy myself for a few days. Now I would need to redo my schedule.

The next leg of my journey would take me to Dallas/Ft. Worth, Texas. Along the way I found another small RV park. This park had all the amenities, including cable, water, electricity, and a place for me to walk my dog. I stayed there for a couple of days and would make sure I mark this place on my map for future overnight stays.

When I arrived at my next stop, I checked in for the next four nights. After settling in, people asked me about the pictures on the side of The Wine Cellar RV. I was talking with some people about wine cellars for about an hour, I found that it was getting late and I wanted to just relax.

Later I was asked to join a neighbor for a glass of wine. They served a good cabernet. Everyone was always surprised to see the wine glass I would bring over. It is crystal, and everyone says to me, "Aren't you afraid of breaking it?" My answer is always no.

I received a call the next day from one of the local TV stations. The article had just come out about me in *Maverick Magazine*, a Ft. Worth magazine. I went to the station for the interview, but they ran out of time. Oh well, better luck next time. The reporter took all my information and said that the next time I come through their town I should give him a call.

Texas is a long state to travel across. This state is about one thousand miles across and seems to go on forever. There is nothing to look at for miles and miles. Torrey hesitated to go outside since he got burrs on his feet the day before and limped back to the RV looking pathetic. I wound up stopping in El Paso for Thanksgiving Day. The local Fox station did an interview with me. I stayed around a day to see it, but it aired the day after I left. I tried to find it on their website. They had told me that a news company does their links. I called them, and they wanted a lot of money for the link. I will never see, it I guess.

AT&T cellular company had finally done the one thing that would cause them to lose my business after almost forty years. I had received a warning that they were going to suspend my Internet service because I was getting close to the 5 GB limit. This was the third time I had received this e-mail from them, although I had always had unlimited service on the Internet with them. All of a sudden they were telling me that they didn't sell that package anymore. I did not understand, because the package that I had with my cell phone was not a service they sold anymore either. But this was "grandfathered in," as they put it. It was going to cost me an arm and a leg if I stayed with their service.

I decide to with another carrier and called Verizon. It took three days of hell to get everything changed over to Verizon. Nothing ever goes right when you are told, "It will be easy; don't worry." Finally, after the three days, I was able to have phone service again. Now if I could get an Internet provider for my computer, I will be happy. It took another couple of days to get everything in order again. A lot of people did a lot of things to make it all happen, and my thanks go to all.

When traveling across the state of New Mexico on Interstate Ten one morning, my eye caught something I had never seen in my life—a rainbow where you could actually see both ends. I wanted to get off the road and follow it to see if there was a pot of gold at either end. My luck would have been that I would go to the wrong end first. Then by the time I would get to the other side, it would either disappear or there would no gold there either.

The other thing I found interesting in New Mexico was a giant roadrunner. If Wyle E. Coyote had seen this one, he would have had to have the Acme Company ship him a much bigger trap.

Both ends of the rainbow

Giant Roadrunner

An interview with Steve Dela Duca

As wine drinking has become more popular in the United States so has wine storage. It seems there are a lot of bottles piling up in areas where wine should not be stored.

But dedicating wine storage to a particular room isn't just for the rich and famous. Sometimes it's not even a wine cellar; it could be just a stand-alone unit.

And the idea of wine cellars has grown over the years. Some homeowners want a wine storage area installed even before they start collecting wine.

Even in today's economy, you still have mega-kitchens, huge bathrooms, home theaters, and spas that are assumed to be standard. Some builders are always looking for new areas to add to a home to attract buyers. Wine cellars fall into this category.

I spoke with Steve Del Duca of American Classic Wine Cellars. He told me that many people were reluctant to uncork an expensive bottle of wine, much less build a space to store it. That changed in the mid-'90s as people became more aware that wine does have health benefits. "About ten-fifteen years ago, wine was really an enigma," he said. "People didn't understand it because it wasn't part of our culture."

As people started to drink more wine, they were also starting to figure out which wines they most enjoyed. So now they wanted to start collecting those wines. They soon found out that a certain vintage wouldn't be available as readily as their favorite soft drink. Now people needed a proper storage area with the correct temperature, and humidity became necessary for aging wines and protecting their collection. Some homeowners were willing to spend tens of thousands of dollars creating wine cellars and rooms.

I remember doing a consultation with a customer about his new wine cellar. I had estimated the project would cost about $50,000.

I saw that look that I have seen before, but then I asked him an essential question: how much is the current wine collection worth?

His answer: Somewhere approaching $180,000-200,000. The cost was now justified.

So is your reason for creating a wine cellar for storage or entertaining?

Or is it strictly the protection of the wine investment? It could be for all three.

If you are building a new home, this is the least expensive time to build a wine cellar. Retrofitting is always a more expensive option.

Unlike wine cellars built in the old world, modern wine cellars are often more elaborated in their decor. Sometimes they want the wine cellar close to the main living areas for convenience. I have built cellars under stairways, in spare closets, and one time in a garage. I remember one house where a kid's room was converted into a wine cellar. So now when the kid comes home from college, he may never want to leave.

Just remember that when you do get that wine cellar built, think about all the possibilities that you have available today. You can make it as elaborate as you want or just do the basics for now and add on later.

My next stop was Phoenix, Arizona. I stopped off to see another wine cellar company. I moved one of the cellars they had in one design center to another and even put in a new cooling unit for one of their customers. As I cut the new opening, I saw that they had low-voltage wiring for the unit. I told the customer, and of course he said it had been working for years.

Well my comment would be that he was lucky there wasn't a fire. I only put one in; the other one would be installed by someone else.

I then was finally on my way to California. I hadn't been here for about a year and half. Getting out there this time would be a shock. The roads were terrible, and with the state being broke, the future didn't look good. The fuel prices were high, along with everything else out here.

Along the interstate in California I saw a sign for RV parking for $10 a night. *Great,* I thought, *this will be where I kill a few days.* After going around in circles for about an hour, I finally found the RV park. Road construction in California seems to be only at fifty precent The other fifty percent is trying to find your own way. The RV park seemed pretty nice pulling into the driveway.

They told me I had to listen to salespeople give a pitch about the place. That didn't bother me at all. I had an appointment an hour after I got there. Then the salesman told me how great everything was about the plan I was to buy. For only $10,000 now I could enjoy any three days in a row at any one of the RV spots around the country. "Wow" is all I could say. I asked him if there was anything else to buy. He replied that the down payment was only the beginning. For as little as $25-$45 per day I could be assured of any spot without any blackout days. I already belong to another group and could stay pretty much anywhere they were for about $15-$25.00 per night. The only down payment was $40 a year. I told him that as enticing an offer it was, I would have to pass. As I was leaving his desk I looked over to an elderly couple with their checkbook in hand. Must be nice to spend that kind of money in one shot. I spent the rest of my time talking with people and doing the things you do when you are stopped for a couple of days. I was invited to a barbecue that night, and it was great. Of course I brought the wine to drink there.

As I traveled further into California I found that the state had not changed too much in the past two years. Palm trees, desert, and rocks were still a familiar sight along the interstate, and there were lot more people than I remembered. I didn't think going through LA at 10:oo a.m. would be a problem. Where did all this traffic come from? Didn't those people have jobs they should be at? I finally made my way up the coast on Highway 101. The scenery was beautiful. The West Coast is always great to look at—the waves hitting the rocks, those whitecaps as they roll into shore. You can sit there for hours, just looking at the tranquility; you are almost in a trance. Then you realize that you are still driving your RV down the road at sixty miles an hour.

After getting to the jobsite in Windsor California, I found out the the wine racks were not yet delivered. No big surprise here, especially when the customer knew I am making the trip from the midwest just for them. It was not a total loss.

Celebrity Wine Review TV invited me to an event at Jacuzzi Winery on Saturday night. I had a lot of fun and met a few interesting people. I even had a chance to meet the most interesting man in the world: the man from the beer commercial, Dos Equis.

Some of the events that I am invited to, Iget a chance to meet some very interesting people. This one is where Charity Winters from CWRTV is interviewing the most interesting man in the world.

I always try to be around some beautiful women. This is Jessica from Wine Channel TV.

I had an interview with *IWA Magazine* on December 21, 2010. I went on camera talking about wine cellars and some of the dos and don'ts of cellar building. They took pictures of some of my famous wine cellars in The Wine Cellar RV This will be aired on IWA Magazine website, January 2011

Next I traveled back to The Ritz Carlton Residences at Singer Island, Florida. The wine room is small but quite unique. The wine room will house about five hundred bottles. I used redwood racking for the main bottle count of about four hundred-plus flanked by about seventy bottles of metal racking to either side. The room is an angled room with glass doors to view the entire collection. Soft lighting coming down from the ceiling to glisten off the wine bottles will make you want to just keep staring at the new wine room.

Redwood racking with metal racking accent

As you can see it is a small but very effective wine room. These condos are renting year round, and the view from up there is great. This wine room took, from the time I got there to the time I left, about six hours to create. Don't think just anyone can do this; remember that I am The Master Wine Cellar Builder. As I walked around this condo, I was thinking that this would be a great place to spend the winter, sitting out on the balcony sipping wine, looking out over the Atlantic Ocean, going down to the pool, or just relaxing. Maybe after doing a few more wine rooms here I would be able to come back as a guest. I was always looking for a place to spend the winter. I wonder if The Wine Cellar RV would draw attention being parked there a while.

Now that I was done with this job, it was off to California again. Be sure to look for the bus along the most southern route of the United States. When you see us, say hello!

This week I was at Kunde Family Estates installing racking from floor to ceiling in their VIP room. This job was one of those jobs that you would imagine would go rather quickly. It had about a six-hundred-bottle count, but then you add the fifteen cabinets, one arch, and ten rows of lighting. Well, you get the point that it took me a while to get done. Then throw not enough material into the mix and you could have a disaster.

When I started out on this job, I did my normal routine. I would lay out everything for easy reach. Then I got to one point the next day and started to wonder why I didn't have enough parts. I looked in every box, figuring that someone had just misplaced some of the parts. I spent the better part of the day looking for something that wasn't even there. Finally I called the factory back east and explained my dilemma. You see my problem was that I had a five-count display row with only enough parts for a four-count. When I talked with the manufacturer, he told me that this was only made up for a four-count display and that I must be looking at it the wrong way. Even the plans that were right in front of me stated only a four-count display. I sent them pictures to prove I wasn't crazy, and they sent me the new parts to finish the job. Since this was dark-stained with a clear coat finish, it would be a few days before I had my parts. I got the rest of the material a couple of days later. They did a great job in getting it out for me.

In the meantime I started on another job there in wine country, which should have been an easy job also. But it was not the case this time either. This was one of those jobs where the measurements were off by just enough to make life a challenge. You see my racking was 98 1/2 inches high and my room was 97 inches high. See the problem? After cutting the new height to all racking, everything was going smoothly until the width of the room came into play. Concrete walls have no give to them whatsoever. This goes back to what I always say: "Make sure all your measurements are correct." The factory can't guess height and width of your wine cellar. So when those mistakes are made, you need a wine cellar builder who knows how to fix things. Also, for those people who will have future wine cellars measured, make sure your guy has that tape measure in three to four different places on the walls and ceiling height. On this wine cellar I just shook my head and did what I do best.

Next I went back to Kunde Vineyard and got ready to install the rest of the racking. I had to wait all day for the floor guy to get the rest of his floor in, and while I waited I enjoyed some of the great wines offered at

Kunde Family Estates. I need to be careful not to drink too much, as I still need to work off a ladder. These racks were about twelve feet from top to bottom. Working where the public is always interested in what you are doing is both good and bad. You get a lot of compliments on your work, and a lot of questions also. Of course this slows down the progress.

I parked The Wine Cellar RV on the property of Kunde Family Estates, and they were kind enough to let me spend the night here. When I woke up in the morning, the vines, even though bare at the time, were simply a beautiful sight to behold while drinking that first cup of coffee. This is an experience few people get to enjoy—seeing the sunrise over the hills, looking at the vines that were now dormant, just waiting to bear fruit. Will some of this wine end up in a wine cellar that I had already built? Or will some of the wine be sitting back and be shipped to a wine cellar that I had not yet designed?

Racking at Kunde VIP Room

The racking is redwood with a dark stain and then covered with a poly coat finish. This is about as close as you can get to have your racking look like furniture and not pay the furniture price. Trust me, it is not inexpensive to do it this way either. But when it's all done, the racking looks great. The very top row of this design boasts of displaying magnum and jeroboam bottles. The next section is for individual bottles and has room for 7.5 mil wine bottles. Moving to the next section there is a back-lit arch flanked by five display rows on either side with high cabinets to hide all the stemware and plates. The very bottom has a dishwasher and a wine chiller along with more cabinets.

Kunde Family Estates is sitting on about two thousand acres. I had a chance to taste some of their wines while I was "working." The 2007

Reserve Century Vines Zinfandel was one of those wines I really liked. Here is the comment from Tim Bell, Winemaker:

> "Each year the historic Shaw Vineyard at Kunde Family Estate forms the heart of our Reserve Century Vines Zinfandel. Over time, the gnarled vines have formed beautiful abstract sculptures, a true collaboration between nature and man. In 2007, our 125th harvest from these magnificent stalwarts, we knew we had a wine that was truly special. With flavors of raspberries and dark chocolate, this wine is like drinking liquid velvet. The restrained use of new oak in aging has enhanced the mouth feel and protected the luscious fruit flavors. History never tasted so good!"

This is part of what happens when you have a motor home going down the road and bouncing around on the highways. I was in Santa Rosa for a couple of wine cellar jobs. One morning on the way to a job, my steering didn't seem to be working as it was supposed to. I went to the auto parts store to get some hydraulic fluid for the system. I filled it up, and my steering seemed to be back to normal. I got about a mile away from the job when I noticed a stream of fluid coming from under the RV. Pulling over to the side and looking at the fluid, I saw that it appeared to be the same hydraulic fluid I just put in. I couldn't go to the customer's house with all this oil coming out.

I got on the phone and explained my situation to a couple of shops. Everybody was too busy to see me. Finally, after talking with about eight shops in the neighborhood, I got a shop in Winsor to look at it. They said it was overfilled and removed some of the fluid. I drove around town a little while before I took off on my next journey. I saw oil on the back of the RV and just dismissed it as some of the oil from the previous leak. I got about three hundred miles down the road and heard a grinding noise coming from the rear. I was about a half-gallon low on fluid. Filling it up, I made it to my destination in San Diego.

Concerned about the RV, I made an appointment with the local Cummins dealer referred by Spartan, maker of the chassis. They looked at it, and I got the bad news. I needed about $3,000 to fix all that was wrong. Now I was doing what most RV people hate to do. I was sitting there waiting for the parts to come in. Then it gets worse: you wait at the dealer to get the job done. Since this is an all-day job, I would have to find something to do. This is the life you have when on the road. It's not really any different than the person living at a house. Things break and you have to fix them.

There is also a sad side to traveling around the country. The economy has had an impact on a lot of people, me included, and some of the things that you see around the country show that people do what they need to do to survive. People have been forced out of their homes and onto the streets. Some of these people turn to the cheapest way of living, which sometimes wind up be an old trailer in an RV park. They now have an affordable place to live. It's not that 1,000-1,500 square foot home but a modest 200-300 square foot trailer. It's someplace to call home. Some of these people are forced to live in tents and don't have the modern conveniences of indoor plumbing. They rely on other people's generosity and good will. I found that to be the case for some people living behind a truck stop in Salina, California. I stopped to get fuel, and when I let my dog out for a break, I saw tents where the people lived. Now I know what you are thinking that people living on the streets isn't a new thing, but it is more common now than ever before.

There are three people living in these two tents.

One time I was traveling through some of the back roads of Ohio. As I drove down this two-lane road, the traffic started to back up a little. I thought it was just a farmer on a tractor going from field to field. As I got closer, I was surprised and amused by what I saw in front of me. It was a farm tractor, but in this case it wasn't used for any farming. The banner on it says it all.

Farmers take to the streets

This is what you get when you stop at a winery in Texas. Not only do you get to taste some great wine, but people are always asking about what you do. Sometimes they want their picture taken.

It was cold that day in Texas, but the women were hot.

As I traveled around the country, sometimes things came up that I didn't figure on. One Saturday morning I needed to go to the grocery store to stock up. When I came out of the store, a man came up to me and asked me about the pictures and signs on the RV. We talked for a little while about wine cellars and movie stars. I found out that he knew a couple of the stars himself. The town high school was having a car wash to raise some money and asked me if I would let them wash The Wine Cellar RV. Since it was for a good cause, I said sure. There must have been ten people around the RV washing it. As I watched them I saw other cars get in line. A few of them said they saw this RV with pictures on it and got in line. So I think that maybe I helped them raise a little bit of money that day.

Helping a local high school to raise some money for their team

Sometimes things you see from the window of The Wine Cellar RV are just beyond words.

There are no words for this.

Sometimes the things you see are quite interesting. Like this scene at Harrah's Casino in Maryland Heights, Missouri. There was a car fire on the first floor of the parking lot. There must have been a dozen emergency vehicles on the scene. When there is a fire or incident at a casino, it can be a major catastrophe.

St. Charles, Patton Ville, Maryland Heights, and a few others responded.

My dog is always ready to go. Sometimes I think he even wants to drive. I would let him if his feet could reach the pedals.

My dog Torrey

I manage to make new friends all over the country, sometimes they invite you to their restaurant. As this was the case with Chef Dallas of the Tenth Street Restaurant in historic San Miguel, California.

In front of the Tenth Street Restaurant

When in California, always watch out for the big people. I have seen them in Arizona before. This is the first time I have seen them in

California. They are always standing guard over the fields. (They are made of cardboard)

They usually just hang around the fields.

One week I traveled in the Wine Cellar RV from the West Coast to the East Coast. My journey started in Santa Rosa; this is wine country. As I traveled on some of the back roads through Napa, I wondered when I would have all the time I needed to have the opportunity to taste some of the great wines that were just harvested. As I looked out the window, I felt that I had one of the best jobs. I get to drive around the United States, drink great wines, visit some of the finest homes in the nation, and get a chance to meet some of the stars, celebrities, and all the other great people in this nation.

Making my first stop for the night, I retired to a little place in Buttonwillow, California. As I was outside with my dog, a man walked up to me and asked me if I was with Celebrity Wine Review TV. Looking at the logo on the RV, I said yes. He said a friend of his had told him about us, and then he asked what I did. I told him I was the wine cellar expert. He had told me that he liked the information that he had read on wine cellars. One day he might be able to afford one. The last thing he said was say hello to Charity Winters, (The Host of Celebrity Wine Review TV).

My next stop was in Phoenix. I had spent the night at one of their local casinos. When I was out walking my dog around, another man came to me to tell me that he got CWRTV e-mail and thought it was great. When he found out that I wrote about wine cellars, he asked me a lot of questions. I was almost late for my meeting in Phoenix. He told me that we should keep up with all the great stories and interviews. The last thing he said was "Tell Charity hello for me when you see her."

It was great to talk with people about wine cellars and wine. Traveling from state to state, everyone had a different point of view about what they would like to have. One person I spoke with told me that he just wanted a place to go to and smoke a good cigar while drinking his wine. When I told him that smoking in the wine cellar wasn't the best thing for the wine, he just looked at me like I was crazy. After I explained to him that wine doesn't like to be disturbed by odors, including fine cigars, he understood. Talking about cooling systems, racking, and the construction of the room gathered more interest. I hope that anyone interested in building a wine cellar will call an expert. I told people I met on this trip to look up the ten questions to ask your contractor, written by me and published by CWRTV.

As I traveled along the bottom of the United States this trip it was very cold. The temperatures ranged from the twenties to the fifties—not very warm this time. As I stopped to let my dog out for a walk in a rest stop, I encountered a man standing next to The Wine Cellar RV admiring the pictures on the side. He turned and looked at me and told me that he knew this RV and started telling me about The Master Wine Cellar Builder, traveling around the country. I just kind of smiled until the light came on over his head. Then, turning a little red in his face, he said to me, "This is you, isn't it?" I said yes and asked him if he wanted to see the inside of the RV. He took a few pictures and even asked a stranger walking by if he would take a picture of the both of us. This made me feel like a celebrity that day. I am glad people do pay attention to some of the things being written about wine cellars. He said he would subscribe to CWRTV. He was really happy to get a bottle of wine from me. There are so many nice people that you run into across in this country; it's hard to believe we have so many bad people also.

It's great to ride around the country and find that everybody wants to take your picture (and a shot of The Wine Cellar RV of course). Traveling from San Diego across the southern route of the United States, I stopped off at a place called "Chuys" in the middle of West Texas. This is the stopping place for many great people, such as John Madden, Johnny Cash, and many other stars who have passed this way on their journey. The Dallas Cowboy Cheerleaders have also graced this restaurant. John Madden first ate here in 1987. He enjoyed the food, as I did, and has come back every year since then. Whenever I travel out Interstate 10 through Van Horn, I definitely make this a stop for some great Mexican food. They took a picture of The Wine Cellar RV and now will have a place on the wall along with the great stars that visited before me. Before I left they had given me a t-shirt to put on my wall of fame in The Wine Cellar RV.

Chuy's T-Shirt

I also autographed a bottle of wine for them to place along with the picture of the Wine CellarRV.

I had one of their specials for lunch and did not need have to eat for the rest of the day. The portions were very generous. When you travel across West Texas and are hungry for some great Mexican food, stop in at Chuy's and tell them that John sent you and look at all the pictures of stars on the walls. Don't forget to gaze at the picture and wine bottle from The Wine Cellar RV and make a big deal over it.

The second part of my story is about a ghost town west of the Dallas/ Fort Worth area. I had seen this place many times from the RV as I traveled along Interstate 20. This time I had the time to stop and talk with the people at the Smokestack Restaurant.

Smokestack Restaurant

The restaurant is in the town of Thurber, Texas, population five—yes, I said five. It was one of the first cities in Texas to be totally electrified. This town was fueled by coal, built by brick, and drowned by oil. When oil was discovered in the nearby town, Thurber just about died out. By 1930 it was a ghost town. The building that holds the restaurant was built in 1890. The smokestack appeared in 1908. Currently the restaurant is owned and run by Andrea Bennett and her son Rusty. They have had people coming in for lunch and dinner for the past forty years. For an eating establishment to be in business for that long is an accomplishment in its own; not to mention that it is also out in the middle of nowhere.

I had a chance to speak with some the patrons having lunch at the Smokestack. I asked them to tell me about their favorite dish. The response was "It's all great." I was treated to the specialty, chicken fried steak smothered with gravy. This recipe had been handed down from a few generations, I was told. The side dishes were mashed potatoes and a giant roll. They also served some breaded fish for my enjoyment. Then they topped it all off with a piece of pie that was simply beyond words. I didn't go in there for lunch; I just was interested in the story about the smokestack. I always get free lunches, dinners, and wines no matter where I go. It would certainly be rude for me to turn them down. I do like my job very much.

So when you find yourself wanting to just pull in and get that plain hamburger and fries while driving through West Texas, remember the Smokestack Restaurant for breakfast, lunch, or dinner in the ghost town of Thurber, Texas. Of course don't forget to stop in to see my friends in Van Horn, Texas, for a great Mexican meal.

Getting down into Florida I found that the weather hadn't changed yet. But in a few days the temperatures would rise. My wine cellar to be built in West Palm Beach should be ready for me to the next Thursday. I would be right next to the beach; with any luck it would be warm enough to do some sightseeing, heh, heh. But it didn't look like the weatherman would cooperate and tell me what I wanted to hear.

Four hundred-plus bottles

The cellar pictured here is a redwood accented by metal racks. This is a great look for a contemporary design. This is a wine room as opposed to a wine cellar. And if you read the earlier posts, that I had talked about in articles at Celebrity Wine Review TV, you know the difference I refer to. This is a great use of a small space off the dining room. You can enjoy dinner while viewing your wine bottles glistening in the light.

Did you ever have a bully who made you a little leery to walk down the street? Or maybe not be able to go to your favorite restaurant? That's what happened to me in the parking lot of Harrah's Casino. I am not talking about when I was a young boy either. I was a grown man with an apprehension of walking across the parking lot without a cane or an umbrella in my hand. Yes, one day when walking across the parking lot of Harrah's Casino with my dog next to me, I was bullied into going back to the RV. All I was going to do was put some trash in the trash can. My bully stood there in front of me daring me to walk by him. His chest stuck out, and he started yelling at me. My dog even got out of the way. Torrey stood behind me and expected me to protect him from our bully. I high-tailed out of there and went back to the RV to regroup. Leaving Torrey in the RV, I knew I had to face my bully or I could never walk across that parking lot again. I walked across the lot with an umbrella in hand, ready to face whatever would come up. As I walked to the other side, there it was! As I got closer it started toward me, and I knew what I had to do. Its feathers started to spread, and now it was honking at me. You see, my bully was a goose protecting an egg or something in the immediate area. As the goose came toward me honking and raising hell with me, I hit it with a bag of trash. As I looked at my bully square at its open beak, I knew I had not won the battle, but it went off to the side and let me through. Walking across the parking lot, I could feel those two little beady eyes on me and I kept an eye on that damn goose as I walked around.

My parking lot bully

One of the places where I always stay when in St. Louis is the Sundermeier RV Park in St. Charles. There is a double treat at this park. It has a great RV park and is home to Beef Eaters Restaurant. Both places have been visited by many of the local celebrities. The park has won the "RV Park of the Year" award several times.

This RV Park has several amenities to enjoy while here. Not like some of the parks around the country, this park has level concrete sites, along with cable TV, free wifi, and a meeting place for all your gatherings. They are close to the casinos and shopping and within an hour of some of the great wineries in Missouri. If hiking or riding a bike is your thing, the Katy Trail backs up to the park. Bring a lunch with you; more than likely you will make a full day of it. Along the trail in St. Charles, there are bars, wineries, and eating establishments for you to visit along your journey.

Beef Eaters Pub & Grill

If you just plan to stay in the park and don't want to cook, you might visit the restaurant that is enjoyed by all: the Beef Eaters Pub & Grill, right on the property. They have the best prime rib I have eaten in a long time; pair it up with a loaded baked potato, a great salad, and of course some home-grown Missouri wines. It with certainly will bring you back time and time again. So remember when you come through St. Charles, in your Prevost or your pop-up trailer to be sure to spend the night or the week at Sundermeier RV Park. You will get the celebrity treatment—I know I do.

Now that you have decided that you will have a 1,500-bottle wine cellar, you have to decide what kind of racks you are going to use. My personal opinion is that I like *redwood racking*, whether custom or kits.

It will last a *lifetime,* and isn't that what you are looking for? The kind of redwood you will decide on will affect the cost. You can choose either heart redwood or premium redwood. The premium redwood will give your wine cellar personality. It is not a solid color and is a lot less expensive than all heart redwood. That way you can spend more money on wine. Makes sense, doesn't it? If you look at my video you will see some of both (http://www.youtube.com/watch?v=FkIkbi82P9Y).

If you decide to go with kit racking, seen in the photo, as opposed to custom racking, that's great. You can make the designer kits look like custom racking if you know what you are doing, and at a lot less cost. I have been recommending kits to people for years. This is the less-expensive end of wine racks, but with all the trim that is available today, those kits can be made to look like a custom cellar. I have done quite a few over the years like that. When you have a custom wine cellar, it will be designed to take up every inch of space. And unless you made very precise measurements, you still may have to cut the racks in the field.

Redwood kits

The builder may have added an inch or so, not thinking that the racks that are ordered are made to fit that exact space. A lot of times I have heard from the client that the factory was at fault when they made the racks. The factory can only make racks for the dimensions they are given. As a **master wine cellar builder,** when I arrive at the house, I have found that rooms have shrunk, and sometimes they even get bigger! At that point you have to modify your racking. Not knowing all the ins and outs of the racking, you could have a hard time making everything look great.

So whether you get *designer kits* or *custom racking*, the variety is almost endless. You can have simple individual racking, diamond bins, case storage, display racks, magnum racks, waterfall racking, vertical display racking, or rectangular racking. As I said, the possibilities are endless.

Marble Floor

The next decision point concerns the floor. What do you want? Do you want ceramic tile, marble or slate, or maybe just to take that concrete floor and glaze it? Or how about a cork floor? I have installed some cork floors that are fantastic. If you have a light floor with dark racking, that is a great look. You can find that look on my YouTube video also. When you install that floor, remember to seal it to the walls. A silicone caulk between the wall and floor will do the job. This is another area where contractors don't look. You are trying to get a tight seal all around the room. Another point to remember is not to install baseboard now. Baseboard will be attached to the racking at the finish.

Custom Redwood Doors

The next step is getting the door for your new wine cellar. It should be an exterior door, well-insulated, and if you prefer a window, make sure it is also an insulated pane. When you install this door, make sure you seal all around the door, both inside and out. The door itself should have a weather seal around the jamb also.

So now we have talked a little about racking, floors, and a door. The only thing that is left is the cooling unit. Depending on the room size, you could go with a unit that could go through the wall or you could go with a split system. A split system needs to be installed by your local HVAC dealer. This has to be installed before the drywall goes up. Any other unit can be installed at a later date. My recommendation is that if you have a 1,500-bottle wine cellar or more, go with a split system. If anything goes wrong with this cooling unit, it could be fixed by your local HVAC company. With any other unit, you may have to send it back to the manufacturer. This will leave a hole in your cellar, although the manufacturer will make every effort to get it back to you as soon as possible.

Now we have covered some of the basics of your new wine cellar. What's left now is to order the racks. When they arrive, call me to install your new wine cellar (www.magnumcellars.net).

One memorable week for me, to say the least, began when I drove in from Knoxville, Tennessee, to do a wine cellar consultation in St. Louis. The room would take quite a bit to make it into a wine cellar. There was a window in the room that they wanted to retain, and the duct work was very low in the room, making the racking and placement of the cooling unit a bit of a challenge. After taking all the measurements and calculating for the cooling unit, my work was certainly cut out for me.

Wine cellar design

In the design I incorporated a small round table in front of the arch. This wine cellar would house around 1,500 bottles, not bad for the space that I had to work with. The racking in this design would be redwood with a light stain (not oil based; we covered that a while back). Some of my earlier articles in, Celebrity Wine Review TV, cover what kind of stain to use in wine cellars. The arch would be back-lit with lead lighting. The quarter-round front shelf would house decanters and wine knick-knacks. This is the kind of drawing that you can expect from a wine cellar consultation.

This week also proved to be a week of moving The Wine Cellar RV to a place of safety more than once. This month in St. Louis gave us rain, hail, snow, and a tornado. The weather in St. Louis gave everyone a roller coaster ride in just a few weeks. A tornado started about forty miles outside of St. Louis, causing destruction as it traveled down Interstate 70 and bearing down on the metropolitan area. At one point it was said to be about three miles wide. It touched down here and there, destroying everything in the path. Houses were ripped apart and strewn about like matchsticks. The tornado ripped through St. Louis International Airport. The airport had to be shut down and reopened about twenty-four hours later, because of the tornado. That was the first time in thirty-plus years that ever happened.

St. Louis tornado

As I drove around St. Louis to see all the damage the tornado had done, I was amazed at the path of destruction in such a short time. The weather bureau had called it an F-4 with a wind force up to two hundred miles an hour. The picture shown here displays what used to be a two-story home. Now it was just a pile of rubble. As I walked around this neighborhood, I talked with the local and national television people. They told me that they hadn't seen this much destruction in quite a while.

The people of St. Louis came together to help their neighbors. Groups of people from the local churches responded to the call. High school teenagers were there to try to help the homeowners gather as much of the personal possessions as possible. It did my heart good to see all this. I went out with a local church to help clear away debris from the houses.

Clearing debris

There were about one thousand people out when I was here. They came from all walks of life to help. The local televisions stations with the help of Red Cross, Salvation Army, and several other charity organizations raised money.

After going through all this bad weather in the Midwest, I was ready to go back to the lifestyle of great wines, excellent foods, and traveling in sunshine. So when you see The Wine Cellar RV on the road, stop by and say hello. It takes more than really bad weather to stop us.

I feel it is important to talk about some bad wine cellar installs. Unfortunately, there are a lot of "wannabe" wine cellar installers out there who may not intentionally take advantage of people but ultimately do! This gives a bad rap for those who are quite qualified in dealing with all your wine cellar needs.

I always talk about doing your homework when it comes to building your new wine cellar. This week I had the opportunity once again to see exactly what I always preach. I can't emphasis enough the importance of building a wine cellar correctly. I have talked about this through the magazines, TV, and radio shows I have been on.

The first question for your contractor should be: "How many climate-controlled rooms have you built?"

The next questions should be: "Can I get some references?"

If either of these questions is not answered correctly, just say, "Thank you. I will find a qualified wine cellar builder."

I went on a service call this week. The only task that I had to do was reinstall some ductwork and make sure everything else ran smoothly.

This sounded good only in theory. I went to the residence, and the owner informed me that the wine cellar had been installed about five years before. We went to look at the cooling system. To my surprise I found that someone had placed both cold air and hot air ductwork in the wine cellar. The cold air coming out of the evaporator was placed on the wrong side of the wall. It was on the bottom of the cellar (note: cold air drops). The ductwork should have been placed near the top. To make things even more interesting, as with any system, whether cooling or heating, you also need to have a return air flow. There was none to be found on this job. The ambient air was going straight into the return portion of the cooling unit, the evaporator was blowing cold air into the cellar, the condenser was blowing hot air into the cellar, and in no place was the air being pulled out of the cellar. It doesn't take a genius to figure out this would not work. To top it all off, the thermostat was hidden behind some racks. *Wow*!

After finding all this with just the cooling unit, I wanted to look further into this wine cellar.

6 mil thick vapor barrier

The picture shows how a vapor barrier should be installed. Inspecting the ceiling of the cellar (only where I could see), I also found the insulation factor was not met. Looking for the vapor barrier was also a challenge: there was none that I could find. So I went back inside and looked at the racking. Hmm, what do I see here—good-looking racking, great storage space, a very workable, eye-appealing design. The contractor did a really nice job of installing the racking.

The only problem I saw was that the contractor had failed to install beam supports. Quite frankly, I am not sure how the bottles above the display racking had held up through the years.

Carpenters, contractors, builders—there are a lot of really great skilled people in this trade. I have run across so many who are true craftsmen. I am not saying that the person who built this wine cellar was not a good carpenter. I am saying that he should have consulted with someone who knows the trade. This is always what I preach.

So if you go back to some of the articles that I have written, you will find the questions to ask your contractor. I don't work on BMWs or Fords, install bathrooms, or build decks—that's where I would call in an expert.

The house is off just a bit!

Would you accept this from the contractor who is building your house? I certainly would not. Why would you let someone whom you do not know build a wine cellar for you? Remember that you are putting a very precious commodity in there: your wines. You want to store them in as safe an environment as possible. Just remember to do your homework before you build your wine cellar. There are a lot of great builders out there.

Pick the one who will do the job correctly. Don't go solely by price , Your wines depend on you to make that choice.

This is the end of this leg of the journey. Be sure to look for us on the road somewhere between here and there. Who knows; we might just be next to you on the road when you look up. Or we could be at your neighbors' house installing that wine cellar.

The Press Discuss The Master Wine Cellar Builder

Sauce Magazine in St. Louis, MO wrote this article about me.

It's white and purple, 40 feet long, 9 feet wide, 12½ feet high and is home, office and workshop for master wine cellar builder John Seitz. But this rather noticeable RV belies the passion and seriousness Seitz applies to the art of building cellars for wine-lovers across the country. And while he says, if asked, that he prefers Cali, Australian, South African and Chilean wines, that's not his biz. Building select cellars is. He's been doing it for more than a dozen years.

Employed and scheduled through The Wine Enthusiast, American Wines and International Wine Accessories, Seitz zigzags the country to meet his clients, and after learning their vino likes and dislikes, he crafts wine cellars that house anywhere from a few bottles to 4,500-bottle collections. And here in his native Gateway City—where he's worked his magic for Ruth's Chris Steak House in Clayton and at the Hyatt Regency downtown—Seitz also teams with Terbrock custom builders.

What if he gets a call from the East Coast while he's dallying on the West Coast having just finished a celeb's cellar? "I hop a plane," Seitz said. For him, his neo-gypsy lifestyle is as compelling as his work.

"I have always had an interest in working with my hands. I love to create. Doing wine cellars gives me that great opportunity." He was the guy who paid attention in woodworking class and went on to building houses. His granddaughter now has the table and chairs he made when he was 10.

"I am constantly training," said Seitz, who won his "master" appellation four years ago after serious hands-on training with major manufacturers on wine racking and cooling units. And it helps to know about wine, he added.

Rendered in redwood, mahogany or oak, a Seitz wine cellar is a custom design with arches, molding, soft lighting, tiled floors, windowless walls, racks upon racks upon racks, and all the tunings to achieve the required humidity and temperature. He's made them big enough to dance in and small enough for a 200-bottle collection. His clients include Fortune 500 CEOs and major sports stars. "I've never built the same cellar twice," Seitz noted.

—Diana Losciale

St. Louis Business Journal—by Greg Edwards

Veni, vidi, vino—St. Louis Business Journal

St. Louisan John Seitz (right) has crafted a niche as a master wine cellar builder to the stars. Traveling coast to coast in his luxury motor home, Seitz has designed and built custom cellars for retired NASCAR driver Rusty Wallace, golfer Annika Sorenstam and the Ghirardelli Chocolate Co. in San Francisco. Locally and nationally, his work can be found at Ruth's Chris Steak Houses. The 59-year-old former homebuilder projects his Magnum Co. will bring in about $100,000 in revenue this year, off from a typical year of $160,000 or more, but better than last year. "Last year was horrible," he said by phone from the East Coast, where he had just completed a cellar for Regis Philbin.

Westchester Magazine out of New York featured an article about me:

Toast of the Town

On the road with master custom wine-cellar designer John Seitz.
Published October 5, 2010, at 10:45 AM
Back in 1995, John Seitz, then a master carpenter/home builder in St. Louis, Missouri, was asked to construct a wine cellar for his friend's home. He did—and his new business was born.
Seitz, today's leading master custom wine-cellar builder, according to *Wine Enthusiast* magazine of Mount Kisco, travels the country in his 40-foot luxury American Eagle motor home, designing and installing each year up to 30 wine cellars for private residences and restaurants. His clients include Regis Philbin, for whose Greenwich, Connecticut, home he recently designed a 700-bottle cellar; retired NASCAR driver Rusty Wallace; and pro golfer Annika Sorenstam. Commercial clients include the Ghirardelli Chocolate Company in San Francisco and Ruth's Chris Steak House.
Seitz's cellars, a prestige item "like a Mercedes or Bentley," are constructed of redwood. "It won't rot or mildew and it will last forever," he says. Floors are typically of ceramic tile, marble, or slate, and walls are constructed from green board, a special dry wall that resists moisture.

Seitz has converted closets and spaces beneath staircases into 200-bottle cellars that start at $9,000. A more typical 1,500—to 1,800-bottle cellar in an 8-by-10-foot space costs about $40,000. "You can put a wine cellar anywhere you put a refrigerator," Seitz says.

For more info: (314) 606-1233 www.magnumcellars.net.

This article came from the *Ladue News Magazine*, St. Louis Missouri.

Wine Cellars

When Taste Reigns

If Robert Louis Stevenson was right, and wine is "bottled poetry," shouldn't your favorite vintages have their own library?

A hand-painted mural sets a vineyard mood in a wine room built by John Seitz
For homeowners who aren't sure where to begin, John Seitz, of the Magnum Company, advises finding a contractor with experience in this type of project. After 20 years as a general home builder, Seitz took his career in a new direction and began studying wine cellar construction. Now, 15 years later, he's built them for celebrities and restaurants from coast to coast and is described by *Wine Enthusiast* magazine as a "master wine cellar builder." He tells new clients that in the beginning, he was "one of the people I would advise you not to use!" Seitz says the addition of a vapor barrier is critical to the proper construction of a cellar or wine room, and omitting it is the most common mistake of inexperienced contractors. "It should be on the outside wall, because it keeps the moisture both in and out, all at the same time," he explains. "Keeping the moisture in helps to maintain the 70 percent humidity necessary to keep the cork moist. If the cork dries out, air is infused into the wine and it turns to vinegar." Too much moisture, Seitz cautions, can lead to mold and mildew, which can also penetrate the cork and cause damage.

Although they are most commonly found in lower levels, Seitz says homeowners aren't limited to that area. "A wine room can go anywhere you want to put it," he says. "I installed one in a fifth-floor condominium." He encourages homeowners to incorporate architectural elements into the design. "Do you have crown molding in your home? Incorporate that into your wine room—it gives a very elegant touch. Consider buying stock tile and breaking it up for a cool mosaic floor. And hand-painted murals can make your space very personal."

Having been called the foremost authority on wine cellars, a lot of my suggestions were used by magazines. I found the following article written by Shirley Anderson.

Hiring a Wine Cellar Builder—7 Tips from a Master

Jan 12, 2011 Shirley_Anderson

Do due diligence when hiring a wine cellar builder. When it comes to hiring a wine cellar builder, be sure to incorporate these 7 tips from a Master when screening potential candidates.

Hiring a wine cellar builder can be exciting because it means that your custom wine cellar is about to be created. When deciding who to use for the job, make sure that you keep the following seven tips in mind to ensure you get the quality you need and want.

7 Tips for Hiring a Wine Cellar Builder—From a Wine Cellar Builder

This advice comes from John Seitz, Master Wine Cellar Builder, so take advantage of his expertise, do your due diligence and hire only a qualified professional.

Question the Builder's Experience

How many climate controlled wine rooms has the builder constructed for other clients? This is important. Wine cellars are expensive and you want only experienced people working on yours.

Get References

Find out if you are able to talk to some of the builder's clients to find out not only how well the work was done but also to learn more about what it's like dealing with the company. If the contractor refuses, seek out someone else for the job.

Find Out About Materials and Installation for Your Wine Storage

You want to make sure that the products (vapor and moisture barriers, etc.) and installation used are correct for your situation and the location of your wine cellar. This is an important enough point that it's worth you doing a bit of research and builder questioning before making a final decision on which company you'll go with.

Know What You Want, What It Does and How to Care for It

Does the contractor use noisy self-contained refrigeration equipment that exhausts hot air? If the installed equipment breaks down, do you have to go through the hassle of returning it to the manufacturer for service? These are things you need to know before hiring someone to build your wine cellar.

Do You Need Extra Equipment to Deal with Humidity in Your Wine Room?

This can be viewed as a bit of a trick question. Ask your wine cellar builder about increased humidity as a result of having your refrigeration equipment installed. If s/he says that you need to purchase extra equipment, don't use that person for your project. Most refrigeration does not increase humidity on its own.

Make Sure the Builder's Insurance Covers Repairs and Issues

If your wine cellar is not properly constructed, mold can develop. If this happens, you want to be sure that your contractor's insurance will cover the cost of remedying the situation.

Discuss Wine Room Details

Will the contractor custom build your racks or use a kit? What kind of door is being installed? These are details that you get to decide but make sure that they are discussed ahead of time, to avoid surprises later on. By the way, you should use an exterior grade door with weather stripping and a threshold.

Thanks to John Seitz, Master Wine Cellar Builder

The information in this article is from Master Wine Cellar Builder and *Wine Cellar RV* host, John Seitz. According to Seitz, if you take the time to do the necessary questioning, research and screening, you'll find a wine cellar builder worthy of your project. Then you can fill your wine room with your favorite vintages and enjoy the fruits of your labor.

The following article was written by the good folks at Ruth's Chris Restaurant in Bentonville, Arkansas.

John Seitz Master Wine Cellar Builder

The man Behind the Cellar If you were looking to build your own customized wine cellar, and called any of the top cellar builders in the U.S., it would most likely lead to a visit from John Seitz. His is the master cellar builder for Wine Enthusiast, Vino-Temp, and Vigilant. His is also the man responsible for the beautiful work done here at Ruth's Chris in Rogers. He stopped in recently after finishing the new Ruth's in St. Louis and I was fortunate to learn some about his line of work.

A carpenter by trade, Mr. Seitz was turned on to the idea of building wine cellars by a friend and has now been in the business for twelve years. I like to think of him as a wine gypsy, as he travels approximately ten months out of the year. He drives from job to job, very comfortably, in his luxury-laden American Eagle motor home.

Once on site, to create a room, John will plan and design every detail. He takes into account what the owner likes to drink, collect, and save as well as the budget for the project. Three to four days after the room is ready, John will go into production, usually installing storage for about

1,000 bottles per day. His attention to detail is meticulous and the end result is always impeccable. The tongue in groove woodwork spanning the walls is as much a work of art as the bottles it will soon store.

John Seitz's work has introduced him to numerous celebrities, professional athletes, and CEOs. He is given the VIP treatment when visiting wineries around the globe and his daily duties often include drinking wine on the job. It is possible that he has found the perfect occupation for a wine lover. John is truly a craftsman who has built a career that is tied to one of his passions.

About the Author

I have been in the building business for over thirty-five years and have worked variously as foreman, superintendent, and project manager on a multitude of construction projects. Before this I ran my own general contracting company, which specialized in restoration and renovation. For many years I realized that there was an unfulfilled niche in my life. When asked by a friend to build him a wine cellar, I knew that this is what I wanted to do. After building wine cellars in St. Louis as a sideline, I decided to put a motorhome on the road to travel from coast to coast to follow that dream. I now travel around the country in an American Eagle motorhome seeing more of the country in a month than most people might see in a lifetime.

Wine cellars, by now, have become extremely popular on both the East and West Coasts and in the Midwest. My company is devoted exclusively to the design, consultation, and construction of custom wine cellars. Now, having built wine cellars for over fifteen years, I am very fluent in the design, construction, and temperature control of wine cellars. I have built wine cellars for stars, celebrities, sports figures, CEOs, and top restaurants across the country.

I was one of those people whom I now preach about in my blogs and articles, telling new clients not to use them. "Don't let your wine cellar be the first one that your contractor builds." I studied with as many manufacturers as I could. I went to their plants all over the country, from Ohio to New Hampshire to California. Many people have e-mailed me, telling me that they saw and talked with me. The wineries and vineyards have treated me as a VIP. I have never had to pay for any wine tasting and am always given a bottle or two, and sometimes a case, to take with me. I always invite people, when I stop, to share the wines that were given to me. When in some of these RV resorts, everyone is always up for a glass of wine with The Wine Cellar Guy.